'Individuals and organizations are either growing or dying. In these disruptive times, there is no stasis. Learning is the key to growth. Alaa and Jeff's work is well-researched and practical. You can apply it straight away to develop yourself, your leaders and your organization.'

Andy Lothian, CEO, Insights Group

'An organization that strives to improve performance must have the ethos of learning at its core. This insightful and practical book acts as a comprehensive guide for leaders to help them develop and embed a sustainable and effective culture of learning into their organization's DNA.'

Russell Longmuir, CEO, EFQM Brussels

'Garad and Gold offer a compelling treatise on the importance of learning and review examples to highlight practices that enable the kinds of collective, organizational learning that our turbulent world needs in abundance.'

Robert MacIntosh, Professor of Strategic Management, Heriot-Watt University and Chair, Chartered Association of Business Schools

'With the nature of work rapidly changing, organizations and businesses need to evolve in new ways if they are to flourish. This timely contribution sets out a clear roadmap to success that will allow organisations to not just survive, but thrive.'

Jamie Cooke, Head of RSA Scotland

'Learning is to do with business and success. Learning is necessary to run a business effectively and at every opportunity, if you see them, to make it a success. The world is changing, and people are changing; Alaa and Jeff have written this book for people to succeed.'

Dr Edward de Bono, psychologist, physician and author of Six Thinking Hats

'Filled with illuminating research and case studies, *The Learning-Driven Business* is an essential in-depth resource for anyone looking to enhance the effectiveness of their business in today's rapidly changing world.'

Angelo Xuereb, Chairman, AX Group

'*The Learning-Driven Business* is both a call to action to firms to cultivate a culture of learning as well as a roadmap for how to do so. In it, the authors Alaa and Jeff have managed to achieve a wonderful balance of theory and the practice. This is an excellent read for practitioners, researchers, executives and policymakers.'

Jaideep Prabhu, Professor of Marketing, Judge Business School, University of Cambridge & co-author of Jugaad Innovation

'This book is a must-read for all top management who do not want their organization to be left behind.'

Dr Ahmed Darwish, Former Minister for Administration Development, Egypt

'Captures various dimensions of learning through the contours of time and space, forecasting the future and bringing it closer to the present. Garad and Gold unravel the power of learning exemplified through compelling management insights and global best practices. It's definitely a much-needed intellectual and practical resource for busy practitioners and researchers.'

Roland K. Yeo Ph.D., strategic HR Advisor, Saudi Aramco and author, Stanford University Press

'An indispensable read on the vital importance of learning – the competitive advantage that organizations and leaders can't live without. Practical and actionable advice for those who want to accomplish more and make a positive difference.'

Dr Palena Neale, Founder, Unabridged Leadership and contributor to Forbes *and* Harvard Business Review

'Individual and organizational learning is absolutely essential to succeed and sustain in a fast-changing world. This book provides a significant contribution to organizational learning and business improvement literature. It is simple and easy to read, with many practical examples of how learning can be applied to create an organizational learning culture.'

Professor Robin Mann, Director, Centre for Organizational Excellence Research & Chairman, Global Benchmarking Network, New Zealand

'To adapt to an ever-changing world, developing a learning mind-set and working in an organization that proactively encourages and invests in creating a learning culture is more critical than ever. Alaa and Jeff have created a very easy to read, comprehensive guide packed full of timely reminders, case studies and practical ways to kick start a sustainable learning behaviour for both individuals and organizations.'

Karen Leftley, President, British Quality Foundation

'In a world of perpetual change, nothing is more important than to talk about innovation, change, creativity and improvement as various kinds of learning processes. A deeper and better understanding of learning in all its forms and locales is well represented in this book which should become essential reading for all consultants, managers, coaches, and teachers.'

Edgar H. Schein, Professor Emeritus, MIT Sloan School of Management, co-author of Humble Inquiry *and* The Corporate Culture Survival Guide

'Alaa & Jeff have astutely provided well-researched and easy to understand insightful representations that can help businesses learn and adapt to changing environments.'

Shane Deniz, Vice President of Product Development & Innovation, MasterCard

'By scrutinizing every aspect of learning, Garad and Gold manage to prove once and for all that learning strategies must be at the core of any organization willing to endure in time.'

Newton M. Campos, Professor of Entrepreneurship & Innovation and IE University Country Director, Brazil

'It's noticeable that innovation is leading to the rise of successful businesses. There is no doubt that the trigger for this is one word: "learning", a concept which the authors expertly deliver through this book.'

Maher Elsherif, Minister Plenipotentiary, Ministry of Foreign Affairs, Egypt

'Learning is one of life's most important endeavours. In *The Learning-Driven Business*, Alaa and Jeff make a compelling case that modern businesses must adopt a learning-driven mind-set in order to survive and thrive. A vital book for leaders who understand the importance of listening and learning and want to embed this into their culture.'

Will Read, CEO, Sideways 6

Alaa Garad
and Jeff Gold

THE LEARNING-DRIVEN BUSINESS

How to Develop an Organizational Learning Ecosystem

BLOOMSBURY BUSINESS
LONDON · OXFORD · NEW YORK · NEW DELHI · SYDNEY

BLOOMSBURY BUSINESS
Bloomsbury Publishing Plc
50 Bedford Square, London, WC1B 3DP, UK
29 Earlsfort Terrace, Dublin 2, Ireland

BLOOMSBURY, BLOOMSBURY BUSINESS and the Diana logo are
trademarks of Bloomsbury Publishing Plc

First published in Great Britain 2021

A catalogue record for this book is available from the British Library

Library of Congress Cataloguing-in-Publication data has been applied for

ISBN: 978-1-4729-8667-2; eBook: 978-1-4729-8665-8

2 4 6 8 10 9 7 5 3 1

Typeset by Deanta Global Publishing Services, Chennai, India
Printed and bound in Great Britain by CPI Group (UK) Ltd, Croydon CR0 4YY

To find out more about our authors and books visit www.bloomsbury.com
and sign up for our newsletters

CONTENTS

Introduction

Have you ever thought about how companies such as Apple, Microsoft and Xerox have sustained excellence over the years? Or why some countries, like Finland, Norway and Denmark, have some of the best public services in the world, keeping them at the top of the world happiness index for decades? Or why some individuals are achieving better results than others? On the other hand, have you considered why 50 per cent of the Fortune 500 disappear every 10 years? Or why some countries stagnate in the same place for decades, sometimes becoming worse in every aspect? It is not only about leadership, not only about people, not about technology and not just about fortune. So, what is it?

It is LEARNING. Learning is the only sustainable competitive and collaborative advantage that an individual, an organization or a government can have. Without learning, we repeat our mistakes and become worse, but with learning, we find solutions to our fundamental problems, especially drastic problems such as Covid-19 or climate change. Learning is needed to facilitate collaboration and partnerships for survival and growth. If we can learn effectively and apply what we learn, we will become better in every aspect. Individuals will unleash their potential and accomplish what they aspire to; organizations will realize their visions and achieve their strategic objectives; government agencies will satisfy their customers and improve the quality of life for their citizens; ultimately, we will become life-long learning nations. The challenge with learning is that it is so complicated because people and organizations learn in different ways and at different speeds. There is no 'one-size-fits-all,' yet we need some guidelines. We need to see some examples so that we can learn from them; we need to know what to do. We believe that people do not mind doing their best, but they need to know what to do.

Learning has become a critical process, but only if it is pursued strategically and embedded operationally in the workplace. The literature and practice have emphasized that learning is a matter of survival; we firmly believe that learning could be an organization's only sustainable competitive advantage. Hence, it is essential to investigate organizational learning processes and how individual learning can contribute towards this. This book therefore attempts to create meaningful structures that define what makes learning by individuals, groups and teams become organizational learning. This book also helps to bridge the gap in the literature about the much-discussed topic of learning and builds upon existing organizational learning theories based on research findings. Our objectives are to:

1 investigate the three levels of learning – individual, group and organization-wide – in order to understand what makes learning distinctively 'organizational';

2 identify the processes and activities used to facilitate and enable organizational learning;

3 examine and explain the perceived association between organizational learning and business excellence.

The importance of learning was never verbalized better than in a quote from W. Edwards Deming, who said, 'learning is not compulsory, neither is survival'[1]. Learning is one of the topics that has been a critical concern across generations since time immemorial. History is full of lessons that can be learned, or could equally be missed, resulting in the same mistakes being repeatedly made. Indeed, people across the globe commonly repeat the same mistakes as both their ancestors and their neighbours. This applies equally to corporations and governments, which seem to like to learn the hard way and get things wrong time and again.

However, there is a light at the end of the tunnel, and this is thanks to the enlightened practitioners, scholars, thinkers, consultants, authors, and business and political leaders who have helped us to open our eyes and start to cherish and promote learning. The result is that nowadays many of us appreciate both conscious learning and mindful learning – the types of learning that make the difference in our lives.

This is fortunate, since learning is the only way to escape our ethical, economic, environmental and social crisis. It could be claimed that learning is the torch that will light our path and lead us out of the darkness.

For, like it or not, every nation on earth is suffering at present – whether due to wars and national disasters, or else terrorism, hatred, injustice or pandemics such as Covid-19. Yet we shouldn't despair; with active and effective learning that leads to a planned course of action, we can reunite and find ways to tolerate each other. And we need to learn how to accept each other. We need to make sense of what is going on around us. The practical approach to this is to invest in learning on all levels – individual, group, corporate, community and government. We need to rebuild, maintain and overhaul our curriculums and educational system to focus on learning instead of teaching.

One of the organizations that has cherished learning and realized its advantages is the World Bank Group. What's more, they've actually taken measures to put learning into action[2]:

'Learning is key to solving development challenges, and to meeting the World Bank Group's twin goals of ending poverty and building shared prosperity. Whether it is food security or Ebola outbreaks, development progress is often challenged by multiple interdependent factors. Mitigating these factors requires change that can be harnessed through continuous learning.'

Learning is inevitable

The idea of organizational learning is not new; it has been present in management literature for decades. However, it only became widely recognized in the 1990s[3], when empirical evidence from 200 large organizations across seven European countries suggested that lifelong learning and learning while at work can be significantly enhanced by the increase of both motivation to learn and the supply of resources[4]. Since then, organizational learning has been a critical process, ensuring the very existence of whole industries; without organizational learning, entirely new products and industries would not have been spawned[5]. Despite the importance of the topic, though, there seems to be a lack of consensus regarding the relevant definitions and the methods of practising learning within organizations. Indeed, learning can be perceived in a variety of ways: acquired knowledge, understanding, a change in behaviour or a revision of attitude. It also may, or may not, lead to an improvement in performance[6].

We said earlier that learning is inevitable for every organization, whether private, public or non-profit, and that learning may be the only sustainable competitive advantage that an organization can have. In fact, the hallmark of effective organizations can be their capacity to learn. It is therefore not surprising that learning has become a focal point for competitive advantage. A group of researchers has put together a declaration on learning, where the central idea is that:

'Learning can be the most vital, engaging, and enjoyable aspect of our personal and collective experience. Equally, learning can be difficult, and the source of much of our pain and failure. The ability to learn about learning and to harness the learning process is the key to our ability to survive in a complex and unpredictable world.'[7]

We embrace the ethos of the declaration on learning summarized in the above quote which we apply to this book; it draws on our 2019 paper, 'The Learning-Driven organization' (LDO) – a publication that established a holistic approach for helping businesses to apply the concepts and mechanics of organizational learning (OL). LDO covers all the various levels of learning: individual, leadership, team, organization-wide and machine learning. It therefore caters for stakeholders in any organization, such as shareholders, customers, employees, regulators, society etc, as do the organizational learning mechanisms covered here, which offer a wide range of advantages to businesses and their stakeholders. This book is informed by evidence from research and builds on a review of an enormous number of documents, records, manuals, emails and guidelines (more than 3,000 artefacts).

The book comprises four parts. Part 1 addresses individual learning aspects and mechanisms and consists of four chapters:

FIGURE O.I   The Architecture of the Learning-Driven Organization

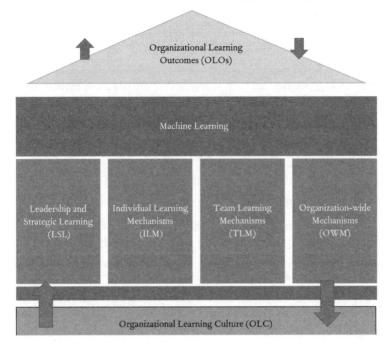

Source: Developed by the authors

+ Chapter 1: Leadership and Strategic Learning
+ Chapter 2: Reflection
+ Chapter 3: Mentoring and Coaching
+ Chapter 4: Employees' Cross-training

Part 2 addresses topics such as:

+ Chapter 5: After-action Reviews (AARs)
+ Chapter 6: Problem-solving Teams (PSTs)

+ Chapter 7: Action Learning Sets (Learning Circles) (ALS)
+ Chapter 8: Futures and Foresight Learning

Part 3 examines the mechanisms of organization-wide learning:

+ Chapter 9: Machine Learning
+ Chapter 10: Benchmarking
+ Chapter 11: Feedback Loops
+ Chapter 12: Self-assessment
+ Chapter 13: Quality Awards
+ Chapter 14: Suggestion Systems
+ Chapter 15: Dialogue in the Learning-Driven Business
+ Chapter 16: Mystery Shopping and Auditing

Part 4 brings it all together and draws conclusions:

+ Chapter 17: The Learning-Driven Organization Model
+ Chapter 18: Conclusion: The Way Forward

We are pleased to have written this book for your education and enjoyment and we welcome feedback, ideas, critique and your own stories.

Yours in learning
Alaa Garad & Jeff Gold
May 2021

Part One

LEADERSHIP LEARNING AND INDIVIDUAL LEARNING – INTRODUCTION

+ Chapter 1: Leadership and Strategic Learning
+ Chapter 2: Reflection
+ Chapter 3: Mentoring and Coaching
+ Chapter 4: Employees' Cross-training

In this section, we consider fundamental aspects of the Learning-Driven Business (LDB), all of which are underpinned by the process of learning. We recognize that learning can be perceived in a variety of ways: acquiring knowledge, enhancing understanding, changing behaviour or revising one's attitude. At a fundamental level, learning is the enhancement or transformation of an individual's mental models based on newly available information. In simple terms, a mental model is a set of deeply ingrained assumptions or beliefs in one's mind. What is essential to understand is how individuals throughout a business can become the source of ideas and practices that, through interaction with others, become accepted by everyone in the workplace. It is for leaders to harness such learning, and this is why in Chapter 1 – Leadership and Strategic Learning – we emphasize the role of leaders in forming, executing and reviewing strategy. We also highlight why they have to be critical thinkers in this work. In Chapter 2 – Reflection – we focus on the need for leaders and others to explore the meaning of their experiences and how they interpret them so that they may become autonomous critical thinkers. We show how people can consider the patterns of their thinking so that they become aware of assumptions that can prevent new actions from happening.

We see mentoring and coaching in Chapter 3 as crucial mechanisms to create a culture of continuous learning and change. We show how there are key similarities and differences between the two but how, given the way patterns of working have changed in response to Covid-19, there is a need for leaders to use mentoring and coaching skills to sustain visibility and regular relationships with staff and others, even if this is mediated by technology. We argue that this is a major route to creating a learning culture in a business. In addition, as many businesses are likely to face disturbances to accepted ways of working, staff will need to acquire new skills from different business areas and will require cross-training, which we will cover in Chapter 4. Cross-training can help cover absences but also serve as a way for people to develop employable new skills in a time of turbulence and uncertainty.

Leadership and Strategic Learning

On 19 April 2020, the BBC website[8] ran with a headline that posed the question: 'Coronavirus: Will Covid-19 speed up the use of robots to replace human workers?' At the height of the pandemic, it seemed that the so-called Fourth Industrial Revolution (4IR) was about to intensify. As one commentator quoted on the website: '[Covid-19] is going to change consumer preference and really open up new opportunities for automation', citing the fact that robots would not need to social distance while they completed tasks that humans could not do if they were working at home. Thus Walmart in the US started to use robots to scrub floors. Predictions were in place to suggest that, for as long as social distancing remained present in society, the robots' time had come.

Such possible disruptions at a time of crisis are part of a continuous challenge to those who are appointed as leaders and who are given responsibility for the achievement of outcomes in a variety of contexts. It highlights how changes in technologies, processes and practices of organization have presented leaders with a VUCA (volatility, uncertainty, complexity and ambiguity) environment; this requires a response in terms of setting a clear direction for the future centred on complex understanding and agile decision-making[9]. We argue that leaders must engage in learning that is continuous and strategic, that has to include a willingness to embrace critical thinking to avoid what Alvesson and Spicer[10] called 'functional stupidity' whereby leaders can prevent learning and change for the sake of maintaining and sustaining an order that they avoid justifying. In a similar manner, some leaders can be accused of hubris, show contempt for criticism from others and become capable of inflicting damage on their organizations[11].

Leaders, leadership and strategic learning

When we think of leaders and leadership, there is a persistent pattern from research and practice that these terms are synonymous. We are not going to deny the importance of those people appointed to senior positions in any organization as leaders. Nor do we want to deny the many research studies that point to the role of leaders in contrast to managers. For example, leaders establish, communicate and model direction, by empowering and influencing others. They also challenge the status quo and build teams to enact change[12]. Further, there are many models and frameworks that provide leaders with the necessary skills and abilities for the role. One of the most well-known frameworks is the Multifactor Leadership Questionnaire™ (MLQ)[13]. This seeks to measure a leader against four dimensions: transformational, transactional, non-transactional and outcomes. A leader is rated against the elements of each dimension by up to 24 others, who provide 360-degree feedback. The MLQ and the idea of transformational or charismatic-transformational leadership have remained very popular in practice and research, so much so that they have been seen as 'the dominant forms of interest' that reinforce the view of the importance of leaders[14]. Others have suggested that there is limited research to support the idea of transformative leaders, its measurement and use, particularly in terms of impact on organization performance, and that the approach ought to be abandoned so the process can start again[15], but from where?

We are not going to completely abandon the notion of individual leaders and their role in contributing to the LDB. We want to give them a significant responsibility for strategic learning. Now that we have all experienced a global pandemic, this highlights the importance of flexibility and experimentation when it comes to working practices. This has been emphasized through remote working, when engagement is done via video and telephone, the distributed development of work systems and the development of 4IR technologies. These features of life post-2020 point to our inclusion of machine learning (Chapter 9) and futures and foresight learning (Chapter 8) in the LDB model. Both can play a vital role in the production of knowledge in organizations and the need to leverage such knowledge for developing strategy – these are key components of strategic learning[16]. In addition, leaders must become critical and challenge core assumptions that underpin their work as decision-makers. It is important to remember that during the global financial crisis of 2007–09 the learning of leaders in many organizations was highlighted as a failing, in that they didn't take responsibility for what went wrong[17]. In order to avoid another global financial crisis, responsible leaders need to become critical thinkers. Table 1 provides some of the ways to understand critical thinking.

As we will suggest later, there are a number of ways for leaders to utilize this framework of critical thinking.

For most of the twentieth century and into the twenty-first, the primary conception of leaders as the focus of consideration for leadership has held sway. It has become

TABLE 1[18] *Critical Thinking for Leaders*

- ✦ Critique of rhetoric – whether arguments and propositions are sound in a logical sense;
- ✦ Critique of tradition – a scepticism of conventional wisdom and long-standing practices;
- ✦ Critique of authority – be sceptical of one dominant view and be open to a plurality of views;
- ✦ Critique of knowledge – recognize that knowledge is never value-free and objective;
- ✦ Critique of simplification – beyond simple cause-and-effect thinking;
- ✦ Critique of identity – how subjectivity and identity are bound to influence thought and actions as well as emotions.

a 'hot topic' and something of a panacea[19]. Applying for a moment the critique of simplification, seeing leaders *as* leadership makes it easier to attribute success, in terms of linking organization performance to particular individuals, which extends to a justification for significant rewards[20]. However, if for a moment we focus on leadership rather than individual leaders, we might uncover new possibilities. Kelly[21] suggested posing the following question as you enter any organization: 'Where is leadership?' Of course, this will depend on which organization you enter. An easy answer in the case of small businesses might be the owner-managers who have the biggest offices. However, in many organizations, there could be different answers, ranging from particular individuals (not necessarily those appointed as leaders) to groups and teams who exert influence in particular parts of the business. A moment's reflection will reveal that there might be multiple pockets of such influence, all operating in everyday work processes for good or ill throughout an organization and, due to distributed work systems and offsite working, these pockets might not necessarily be within sight of those who seek to make key decisions for the direction of the business. We therefore make a separation between those appointed as leaders and the processes of leadership in everyday work situations. This separation leads to a disconnection and distortion, which we have called the 'leader's conundrum' because leaders still have to make decisions but they are unable to control the everyday processes where leadership occurs.

Such leadership happens in units where individuals work with others and create dependencies between processes. Increasingly, technologies mediate the connections and potentially make decisions – a feature that we consider in the chapter on machine learning.

However, the influence of technology does not mean that leaders need to remain disconnected and, as argued by Gronn[22], they can act as 'agents of influence' if they can engage with the various configurations of leadership. As strategic learners, this is a necessity if leaders are to capture learning from all parts of an organization. For example, this is an example presented by Henry Mintzberg[23] in a famous article in *Crafting Strategy*:

'A salesman visits a customer. The product isn't quite right, and together they work out some modifications. The salesman returns to the company and puts the changes through. After two or three more rounds, they finally get it right. A new product emerges, which eventually opens up a new market. The company has changed strategic course.'

A key insight presented by Mintzberg et al[24] is how making strategy can be a deliberate and purposeful process that passes through distinct phases – formulation, plan, implementation and review – which he called a 'design approach'. By contrast, Mintzberg also considered a 'learning approach' to strategy, which highlights how new possibilities for action can emerge from everyday situations but also from surprises, accidents and other unplanned situations. Much of this occurs through what people are learning from their work but also what machines are learning in their use. Crucially, strategic learning by leaders involves a both/and consideration of the design approach and the learning approach, which we will now consider.

Aligning planning and emergence in strategy

In the LDB model that we outlined in the Introduction, we made it clear that those appointed to the position of leader have a responsibility to provide clarity of direction for their organizations. Accepting that there are many kinds of organizations of different sizes and configurations with varying purposes, the failure to provide a clear direction by the leaders is likely to result in inconsistent communication between and within units, and confusion that can eventually result in deleterious effects on performance and survival[25]. For many organizations, strategy is a nebulous process based on the intuition of key individuals, such as owner-managers, who keep strategy to themselves or, in larger organizations, a staged process that feeds into a single declared document that provides an intent of direction. However, in practice, the organization soon deviates from this direction thanks to certain events and a failure to recognize what is emerging. Our model seeks to correct for such deficiencies. This is vital, given that organizations across the world are facing a future of uncertainty that is likely to continue for many months, if not years. The dynamic engendered by the Covid-19 pandemic has resulted in new ways of living and working and this will continue to unfold. This means that leaders must embrace both designing a strategy and working with learning as it emerges, and they must do this on a continuous basis.

The model has been developed over 10 years, working with a range of organizations that are large, small, private, quasi-public and multinational. In all cases, leaders viewed the process of planning strategy as deliberate and purposeful – to reconcile the gap between perceptions of current reality and desires for the future. It has become accepted that success requires the ability to be proactive in developing an awareness of new factors that were not included in the first strategic plan. In addition, and in response to the difficulties of predicting what will happen over the next 10 years, the anticipation of the future can play an important role in the safeguarding and improvement of an organization by providing clarity to the decision-making process.

The model is shown in Figure 1.1.

FIGURE I.I   Model of Strategic Leading in a LDB

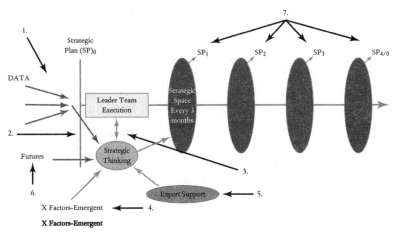

Source: Developed by Jeff Gold

The key features of the model are as follows:

1   Formation of a strategic plan

This is a process of data gathering to identify patterns and trends in an organization's activity and any important developments that need to be considered in a strategic plan (SP). This must include investment decisions, changes in laws and regulations, and responses to environmental and climate pressures. A range of tools can be used when forming a SP, such as strengths, weaknesses, opportunities and threats (SWOT) and political, economic, social and technological (PEST) analyses, and others[26]. Inputs to the process can be taken from different sources, especially where there are different departments and functions operating.

21

In the remote working era, this process can be mediated by digital and cloud technology. However, it is crucial that there is recognition of the importance of talking and interaction between leaders and others. This is a significant point in arguing for and showing the desirability of particular actions and directions that need to appear in the SP[27]. In the LDB, resources that are identified for learning and development activities must be included in a SP to ensure that there is accountability by leaders for implementation and transfer of learning from activities into work performance[28].

2 Ongoing consideration of known issues for strategic thinking

It becomes vital that the process of forming a strategic plan (SP) does not finish once the plan is written. The data gathering to identify patterns and trends has to continue, especially in fast-moving and turbulent times. We advocate the establishment of a particular role, the strategic thinker, to sustain and co-ordinate the flow of data and make sense of it for leaders. In larger organizations, this role can be performed by a manager who can relate to more senior leaders, but in smaller firms, it might be a role for a family member or peer supporter for the managers. Strategic thinking has been identified as a conceptual but holistic activity to make sense of patterns of data that feed into strategy.

Skills also include scanning, questioning, testing and critiquing[29].

3 Leading execution and support for leaders

The outcome of the process of forming a strategic plan (SP) is usually a written document, setting out the direction or intent for actions over a time period – usually three to five years. However, we often suggest to leaders that 'plans are dead as soon as they are written'[30]; they need to be brought to life through execution. We insist that each member of a leader team takes responsibility for at least one strand of a strategy to ensure there are the necessary plans and resources in place for it to be enacted. In addition, the strategic thinker can provide support based on what is appearing from the data and elsewhere and identify problems with execution.

4 Recognition of emergent issues

Support for leaders can also include an awareness of emergent issues that could not be identified in the formation of a SP. Such issues might be unforeseen events that occur after the SP was written (this includes major incidents, such as the Covid-19 pandemic). All have the potential to change, disturb or upset – to a greater or lesser extent – the execution of a SP. In addition, as we identified above, emergent issues can come from within an organization and from the learning of people and machines.

5 Draw upon expert advice for complex issues that emerge
Some issues, such as technological and systems change, projects and cultural shifts, might require help from outside experts, such as consultants, contractors and academics.

6 A futures and foresight group to look 10 years ahead
In Chapter 8, we will consider how the findings from futures and foresight learning (which typically looks 10 years ahead) can provide possible inputs for current strategy.

7 Reviews of strategy every three months
We advocate that time is set aside every three months to review the strategy. The SP sets the direction based on the understanding at the time of its formation. However, conditions can change – the economy slows, markets move and epidemics arise – so the SP can become disconnected from the current reality; this is 'strategic drift'. This can also occur when leaders become trapped in a way of thinking that prevents them from seeing what is really happening. For example, significant retailers in the UK such as Woolworths, Mothercare and BHS failed to effectively foresee or respond to online shopping, and they all went out of business as a result. Strategic drift has been referred to as 'cognitive sloth' that prevents leaders from meeting the organization's objectives[31]. The review therefore serves three purposes:

i   accounting for and assessment of the execution of the strategic plan to identify progress, achievement and shortfalls;

ii   consideration of findings from the strategic thinker in terms of patterns, trends, emergent issues and ideas from the futures and foresight group;

iii   critical thinking for the current strategy to question the direction and underpinning assumptions.

The latter in particular provides an opportunity to consider how assumptions that underpin the behaviours of key stakeholders impact important strategic decisions – a process referred to as strategic assumption surfacing and testing (SAST)[32]. The outcome of these processes allows a revision to the SP so that it better reflects the intended direction and corrects for any strategic drift.

Summary

In this chapter, we have shown the vital contribution of leaders and leadership in the LDB. We made it clear that while leaders cannot be in total control, they still have to provide a direction for others in the business. To do this, they need to work on forming a strategy and becoming critical thinkers in terms of how they review the strategy, paying particular attention to what staff and others are learning and what is emerging in difficult and complex times. We presented our model for strategy making and review, showing the link to futures thinking. Leaders in the LDB must communicate regularly, honestly and with humility if they are to sustain and develop trust with and from others in the post-Covid-19 era and beyond.

2

Reflection

'By three methods, we may learn wisdom: first,
by reflection, which is noblest; second, by imitation,
which is easiest; and third, by experience,
which is the bitterest.'
Confucius (551 BC–479 BC), Chinese philosopher[33]

Introduction

Every organization strives to develop fully engaged
employees who connect their learning to the success of the
organization. Many researchers[34] and practitioners agree
that reflection is a core element and a necessary process
required for organizational learning. Most of the modern
theories promote *reflection* as essential for deep and
significant learning. Reflective learning is defined as 'an
intentional process, where social context and experience
are acknowledged, in which learners are active individuals,
wholly presented, engaging with others'[35]. Learning does

not occur in a vacuum. It is a social process influenced by the social context and conditions; people bring their experience to learning situations. Therefore, learning and knowledge are created within a social context. Reflective learning processes require a form of learning that comes from every part of a learner's experience – familial, personal or practical – recognizing the significance of diversity and of experience. Reflection may lead to a transformation, whereby existing ideas are questioned, challenged and reconsidered, and this is known as 'double-loop learning'.[36] There are four types of theory[37] that allow understanding of reflection:

1 normative theory – states what should be done;
2 descriptive theory – depicts what is going on;
3 interpretive theory – explains why things happen the way they do;
4 critical theory – examines in depth the assumptions adopted in the analysis and questions them.

As we identified in Chapter 1, there is a need for a move towards critical thinking in the Learning-Driven Business. This chapter discusses and answers three key questions: 1. why reflection is greatly needed in today's business; 2. how to reflect; 3. what the expected outcomes of reflection are. It also showcases practical examples and best practice of reflection in action.

The reflective practitioner

In his seminal book, *The Reflective Practitioner*, Donald Schön[38] described two types of reflection and coined the term 'reflective practitioner'. So, what does it mean and how can one learn to become a reflective practitioner? First, we need to understand the two types of reflection and appreciate the importance of this process to organizational learning. Schön identified two types of reflection: 1. reflection-in-action (RiA); 2. reflection-on-action (RoA)[39]. RiA is the process that allows professionals to reshape the situation or activity in which they are working while it is unfolding. It is generally associated with the experience of surprise; Schön suggests that by 'reflecting-in-action', professionals reflect on unexpected experiences and conduct 'experiments' that serve to generate both a new understanding of the experience and a change in the situation. On the other hand, RoA involves reflecting on an experience or situation after it has occurred. When professionals reflect-on-action, they explore what happened in that particular situation, why they acted as they did, whether they could have acted differently, and so on. RoA is often associated with reflective writing, which is when professionals look back on their experiences and examine alternative ways to improve their practice.

The 'reflective practitioners' are the employees who can render some plausible account of how they perform and who can articulate a theory of their practice. Reflection and reflective learning encompass an inquiry process[40] that should be carried out intentionally and within the rules of the organization; organizational inquiry is expected to lead to organizational learning. A reflective practitioner will utilize a repository of understandings, images and actions to reframe a troubling situation and thereby conceive of the action required to resolve the problem. When this occurs, the inquiry results will be manifested in thought and action that are often, to some degree, new to the organization. These novel solutions then lead to new ways of thinking and acting, which consequently lead to improved performance of the organizational tasks. Organizational context and conditions can, however, inhibit useful reflection and inquiry since the attempt to uncover the causes of system failure can be a perceived test of loyalty to an individual's subgroup and can even be an opportunity to allocate blame, exercise avoidance of blame, win credit or prevent others from taking credit. Productive organizational learning[41], by contrast, is the organizational counterpart of what an individual does when he/she engages in reflective practice or reflective inquiry. Therefore, the LDB should be an organization that creates the conditions for individual reflective practice. It is somewhat strange, then, that despite the importance of reflection as a cognitive process of experience examination, it has received minimal attention from researchers studying management learning. As Siebert and Daudelin put it: 'hard data on how managers reflect while engaged in learning is almost non-existent'[42].

Types of reflection

There are three types of reflection:

1 managerial reflection – the cognitive activity in which managers proactively make sense of an experience;

2 active reflection – an activity that contributes to learning during a developmental experience. An internal dialogue involving moments of inquiry and interpretation intends to produce increased insight into experience;

3 proactive reflection – an activity that contributes to learning from a developmental experience; the process of stepping back from an experience to carefully and persistently ponder its meaning to the self.

The three types mentioned above seem to be strongly linked to many researchers' definitions of learning itself as 'the creation of meaning from past or current event[s]'[43]; this is in line with the expected outcome of learning, i.e. leading to a change in behaviour. Organizations need to interpret a purely cognitive process of reflection into actions that affect the organization, or else the learning remains as potential learning (ibid). In his seminal research, Kolb (1984) presented reflection as a form of experiential learning in his four stages cycle, consisting of sensing of experience, reflection on the experience, considering new possibilities for action and then putting any actions into practice – providing for the possibility of an experience to continue the cycle. Allocating time for reflection in and beyond the workplace can be a powerful impulse or spark for questioning the status quo and bringing in new ideas and methods. Therefore, one can easily argue that lack of time for reflection is a major hindrance to organizational learning; such lack of time can be attributed to an organization's obsession with more proactive duties, especially in an environment where action is valued more than reflection. Yet, reflective learning can become a vehicle or enabler for organizational learning because it involves dialogue with others for improvement or transformation while also considering the emotional, social and political context of the learner or the working professional in this context.

Reflection as a catalyst

One of the critical catalysts for the LDB stems from individual learning (IL) and group learning (GL), which in turn is driven by curiosity and reflection on the experience of individuals. From the stage of initiation to the termination of the reflection process, one shifts from a cognitive state to a behavioural state and turns the developed ideas into tangible actions (or they further develop the ideas with other people before initiating action). When leaders create the conducive learning environment and facilitate learning at various levels, organization-wide, individuals will be able to identify areas for further learning and further action. Kolb[44] proposed reflection as a form of experiential learning combined with much focus on individual learning. Some authors[45] argued that Kolb's approach is individualistic and mechanical; it seems impractical, as his approach has looked into learning as an internal process, while social processes are involved in every aspect of learning. Reflection could be internal or external, i.e. thinking to oneself or discussing thoughts with others. We believe that reflection could be utilized as an individual learning mechanism, but this does not mean that it cannot also be a group or team learning mechanism whereby one person shares their thoughts with others, who reshape them. In this case, the process is initiated internally but extended externally, with others. The more an idea is discussed with others, the more it gets developed and shaped; this is an iterative process.

Organizational learning occurs when individuals within the organization experience an incident or a problem and inquire into it on the organization's behalf[46]. Individuals often experience a surprising mismatch between the expected and actual results of action and respond to such mismatches through a process of thought and further action that lead them to modify their perception of the organization or their understandings of a particular business issue. This causes them to restructure their activities to align outcomes and expectations, thereby changing the key ideas for how the business works. This is referred to as its theory-in-use[47].

In order to become organizational, the learning that results from organizational inquiry must become embedded in the perceptions of the organization held in its members' minds and/or in the artefacts, such as policies, strategies, manuals, standard operating procedures, projects and work instruction.

How much reflection?

Reflection becomes more useful when it is deliberately practised, and it requires a clear mind and clear context. To see our reflection in the water, it has to be clear; reflection cannot occur in muddy water. During and following turbulent events such as the Covid-19 pandemic, a period that is defined by uncertainty and volatility, it becomes essential to allocate at least 20 minutes for reflection a few times a week in a suitable environment away from your desk, computer or work area, and while you are in a positive state of mind. Are you at your best in the morning or evening? When is your mind more open and alert[48]? Switch off all background noise and devices to create the best conditions to clarify your intentions and to help you to verbalize your thoughts and feelings.

The best way to optimize the power of reflection is to make it a daily habit. If you usually travel to your workplace, take this opportunity en route, or if you are a frequent traveller, make use of the time spent in airports and in the air. If this does not apply to you, the best way is to do it as you exercise; you thereby gain two benefits: staying fit and having a clear mind to reflect. It's also useful to take notes of your ideas and proposed actions – we recommend using sticky notes (either the paper form or the electronic form on the computer). There are also useful task organizers, such as Evernote® and Trello®; these applications are very helpful and can be used in various ways to jot down reflection outcomes, plan the course of action and monitor progress (this is also a good way to engage other team members or co-workers). They can also be synchronized across both your PC and phone.

The practice of reflection

The learning practices discussed in this book have been investigated in two organizations: LAMAR Hotels & Resorts and Mirage Aqua Park. When working with these clients, we noticed that reflection occurred in several different forms, but mainly via repeated sessions of brainstorming and SWOT analysis. These two informal and semi-structured methods were used across all departments due to their simplicity and the fact that they could be organized without much preparation. In addition, it was found that 'after-action review' and 'post-campaign, post-project reporting' were used interchangeably to refer to reflection.

One of the strategic planning sessions undertaken by Mirage Aqua Park took place offsite over two days and involved all the directors. During the sessions, participants took some time to reflect on an assigned topic, then the same topic was reflected upon with peers, and finally it was discussed and agreed upon by the whole team.

We noticed that reflection was not practised deliberately or proactively in either organization. In other words, it was not institutionalized organization-wide. Instead, it was left to those who are reflective practitioners by nature to choose to do it for themselves. Seeking to better understand this, we talked to employees to find out what motivates them to reflect, how they go about it, and why.

Case study: Mirage Aqua Park
Some of the employees whom we interviewed said that they do not dedicate time to reflect; it just happens when they are fulfilling a task during the day.

> 'I do this on my individual level, and I am always impacted by the book *Good to Great*. I read, and I learn from the business leaders. I try to put this in my daily work. Colleagues are empowered here, and everyone is free to talk without fear of punishment. And we encourage everyone to share their experience with others.' – Linda, team leader, Mirage Aqua Park

As many of the issues are handled during the briefing meetings, new thoughts or suggestions contributed by the employees are channelled either through the suggestion system (see Chapter 14) or during the meetings.

> 'Reflection happens along the day. I mean, I do not sit just to think and find out things, but we are working where ideas come through the daily interaction with everyone.' – David, lifeguard, Mirage Aqua Park

Reflection did not seem to attract much in the way of interpretation of information throughout the organization since it is limited, in most of the examples observed, to a particular department or team. Few cases had an impact overall on the organization. We did, however, witness a few instances where a manager took a decision that resulted in a change in certain policies based on reflection on the current practices.

Case study: LAMAR Hotels & Resorts

Similar to Mirage Aqua Park, reflection is practised in different ways in LAMAR Hotels & Resorts, though mostly on an individual basis rather than in teams, as occurs in an after-action review (see Chapter 5). However, it was noted that some of the interviewees referred to reflection and after-action review interchangeably.

> 'I travel a lot, and the work is always on my mind. I keep thinking while I am travelling on what we can improve

and what goes wrong. So, I have my special way of doing this.'— Samira, senior manager, LAMAR Hotels & Resorts

Not all employees were like Samira. Although everyone seemed to have a positive attitude towards the hotel and its management, many respondents mentioned that once they had finished their job for the day they forgot about the hotel and the work.

'I do not think alone. Actually, we always work and think together as one team. For me, once I leave the restaurant [one of the hotel restaurants] I do not think about work.' — Suraj, waiter, LAMAR Hotels & Resorts

Reflection could be practised in various ways and embedded into other learning mechanisms, such as collective interpretation of benchmarking, SWOT analysis or mystery shopping (MYS), where the management discusses business issues and attempts to spread the knowledge and outcomes from these practices. In this case, reflection is occurring unconsciously. In Mirage Aqua Park, by contrast, reflection is consciously practised during the review and committee meetings, while in LAMAR Hotels & Resorts, the Learning and Development Department seem to undertake reflection on behalf of other departments, i.e. they alone reflect on the incidents and issues experienced and extract the learning lessons in order to disseminate them organization wide.

The theory behind reflection

Back to the theory: It is argued by Lane, Koka and Pathak[49] that there is a positive correlation between prior knowledge and the ability to explore new sources of knowledge. They stated that individuals' prior knowledge influences the locus and efficiency of search for knowledge and new practices; the greater an individual's breadth of knowledge, the greater is their ability to explore new sources of knowledge. Reflection can occur individually or within teams, and it requires empowerment in order that actions can be taken based on the learning outcomes. Reflection can be classified as offline, internal, informal or reactive practice, as illustrated in Figure 2.1, which is based on the classification of four types of theories that explain the nature of reflection, introduced by Burgoyne and Reynolds (1997). Reflection is mainly focused on day-to-day activities and, in the context of the uncertainty caused by the Covid-19 era, such reflection becomes even more critical.

Jack Mezirow[50], an adult education researcher, suggested that reflection can improve a person's understanding of their experience while also allowing for a serious critique. This allows individuals to become aware of and open to the views of others, and to be less defensive and more accepting of new ideas, allowing what Mezirow calls 'transformative learning'. This is essential in the LDB. Through a process of critical thinking, leaders and others can examine feelings, beliefs relating to events and actions, and even the assumptions that underpin them.

Putting theory into practice

One approach is to allow people to reflect on events by writing down two or three paragraphs as stories. This allows them time to make sense of events and any feelings relating to them. The story can be concluded with a summary of the key points, set out as 'I believe' statements. For example, a person may summarize an event by saying, 'I believe I performed well'. This can also occur in strategy review sessions, when the statements can relate to the intent of current strategy. Thus, a team leader can declare 'we believe' statements – for example: 'We believe our customers are loyal'. In both cases, and following a process developed by the philosopher Stephen Toulmin[51], the I/ we believe statements can be called 'claims', which require 'data' or evidence to support them. For example, the claim that 'I performed well' might be based on evidence of feedback from staff or customers, or it might be based on a person's 'gut feeling'. In either case, the claim and data process can begin to bring assumptions to the surface which then can be considered critically.

A further much-needed development is to allow leaders and others in the LDB to collect reflections on events and

FIGURE 2.1   Holistic Reflection

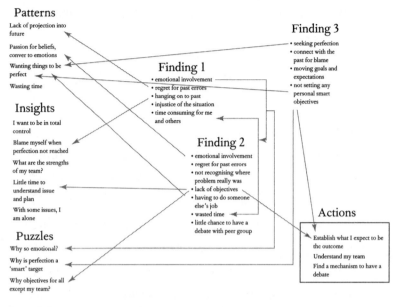

Source: Authors

any critical thoughts and present them as a larger picture or holistic reflection. Figure 2.1 shows how this process worked for a CEO in a service business in the UK.

Figure 2.1 shows how three events were recorded as stories then considered critically. They were summarized on one page and, as they were stated, the CEO began to see patterns emerging from the events, even though different events on different days were being considered. He also could reveal thoughts, insights and assumptions as they came to him during this process. These assumptions were crucial since they allowed new actions to be set as targets, as well as developing questions that needed to be answered.

For this CEO, the process allowed new behaviours to be developed and for him to act as a more inclusive leader.

Summary

Reflection is the cognitive examination of experience. Organizations generally practise reflection, but some should be more proactive in employing reflection and combining it with other practices and techniques, such as brainstorming, after-action reviews and SWOT analysis. Reflection seems to be the essence of learning, and it is the core of the realization process or meaning structure. The organizational learning process is reflective in approach, and most modern theories promote reflection as essential for deep and significant learning. However, it is acknowledged that it could be challenging for organizations to identify the inner activities associated with reflection as it can occur at any place and at any time. The key to success here is for the senior management to appreciate this process, encourage people organization wide to do it, embed it in the management system and support it by providing technology or even a pen and paper that captures the outcomes from such a process.

3

Mentoring and Coaching

'A mentor is someone who allows you to see the hope inside yourself. A mentor is someone who allows you to know that no matter how dark the night, in the morning joy will come. A mentor is someone who allows you to see the higher part of yourself when sometimes it becomes hidden to your own view'.[52]
Oprah Winfrey

Introduction

We perceive mentoring as a supportive relationship between someone who needs advice and guidance and another one who has expertise and knowledge and is willing to provide help and guidance without any conflict of interest. Ideally, mentoring is a long-lasting relationship rather than a one-off exercise or interaction. One of the critical success factors for mentoring is the commitment of dedicated individual voluntary mentors. The key differentiator in mentoring is that it is, and should be, a one-to-one relationship, which permits and contributes towards the development of trust between both parties (i.e. the mentor and the mentee). In order to contribute to the effectiveness of the mentoring process, mentors should be trained in mentoring techniques and learn how to ask questions, give feedback and extract lessons learned. However, we have seen people incorrectly use mentoring and coaching interchangeably. There are determinant differences between both mechanisms, despite their similarities.

Coaching is a popular mechanism for individuals and Learning-Driven Businesses. Most large organizations around the world have some coaching programmes in place. However, there is a lot of confusion around the definition and scope of coaching. We adopt Chapathes'[53] views that coaching is a two-way communication, a reciprocal relationship between coaches and learners, and it has become a necessary technique for performance improvement. We argue that coaching could be one-to-one or one-to-many and it is concerned more with a particular role or profession, which differentiates it from mentoring, which extends to all fronts of life. In this chapter, we will highlight both mechanisms and provide specific examples from practice and research.

Mentoring as an individual learning mechanism

Gregson[54] defined mentoring as 'an attempt to transfer experience and expertise from experienced individuals to the less experienced'. He argued that mentoring in the context of today's business environment is what used to be known as counselling, and described it as a fast-track support scheme where a senior manager oversees a junior colleague who is earmarked for progression. He disagreed with the superficial approach of merely assigning a junior individual to a senior employee in the assumption that the latter will transfer knowledge and experience. This rarely happens effectively if the mentor has not been trained or lacks mentoring skills. Even training may not be enough if the mentor does not have the right skill set and attitude. In the first place, mentoring should be linked to the objectives and goals of the organization. If an organization is unclear about its goals when implementing a mentoring programme, or if the organization's culture is not ready for mentoring, then the mentoring scheme should not be put into operation. A business culture that supports mentoring encourages and empowers its managers to fully develop their staff.

The Chartered Institute of Personnel and Development (CIPD)[55] defines mentoring as a form of training, learning and development and recognizes it as an increasingly popular tool for supporting personal development. Mentoring is used specifically and separately as a form of long-term tailored development for the individual, which brings benefits to the organization. CIPD suggested nine characteristics of mentoring as following:

1 It is essentially a supportive form of development;

2 It focuses on helping an individual manage their career and improve skills;

3 Personal issues can be discussed more productively, unlike in coaching where the emphasis is on performance at work;

4 Mentoring activities have both organizational and individual goals;

5 It is an ongoing relationship that can last for a long time;

6 It can be fairly informal and meetings can take place as and when the mentored individual needs some guidance and/or support;

7 It is more long term and takes a broader view of the person. The recipient is often known as the 'mentee', though the term 'client' or 'mentored person' can be used;

8 A mentor usually passes on experience and is normally more senior;

9 The agenda is set by the mentee with the mentor providing support and guidance to prepare them for future roles.

Why mentors are very important to our success

Mentors can play an instrumental role in the success of individuals and businesses simply because they pass on information, knowledge and wisdom that they have accumulated throughout their experience. They can see areas that require improvement where others often cannot. Mentors find ways to stimulate personal and professional growth and offer encouragement and help keep people going. Another essential characteristic embedded in most of the mentors is that they are disciplinarians who create necessary boundaries that mentees cannot set for themselves. They also act as sounding boards so mentees can bounce ideas off them for an unfiltered opinion. They are trusted advisers and can be connectors and networkers. Having a mentor can help people avoid making the same mistakes beginners make. Above all, these mentors are free, which makes them priceless in multiple ways and genuine in their endeavour[56].

Similarities and differences between mentoring and coaching

Clutterbuck[57] suggested that the key difference between mentoring and coaching is that coaching mainly addresses performance issues related to some aspects of the coachee's life or work, while mentoring is broader and mainly relates to holistic development and career progress. He suggested some commonalities between mentoring and coaching as follows:

+ require and draw upon the helper's experience;
+ be of long or short duration;

+ involve giving advice;
+ work with goals set by the learner or for the learner;
+ deal with significant transitions the learner wishes to make;
+ address broad personal growth ambitions.

Blackman-Sheppard[58] argued that there is an overlap between coaching, mentoring, counselling and consultancy and the boundaries are not clearly identified. A question was raised: is executive coaching a higher grade of coaching, considering that it is tailored to a senior level and high-flying executives? The answer is yes; there are some differences since executives have more sophisticated responsibilities, and they are assumed to be highly skilled individuals who possess a wide spectrum of expertise. A variety of executives use some sort of coaching service, which offers them three key opportunities: 1. time out from the pressure of constant decision-making; 2. confidentiality and safety; 3. detached companionship. Blackman-Sheppard[59] also emphasized the importance of mutual trust between a coach and a learner.

Botmentors and botcoaches: mentoring and coaching in the Industry 4.0 era

Web-based mentoring and online-platform mentoring has become a trend since the emergence of the Internet. For instance, Emelo[60] states that web-based mentoring has emerged with the appearance of social media and using the emerging networking technologies. Some of its benefits are that web-based mentoring gives people the opportunity to expand their network and interact with people with whom they would not normally engage.

Today, e-mentoring – sometimes referred to as electronic mentoring, digital mentoring, online mentoring, virtual mentoring or computer-assisted mentoring – includes any type of mentoring that incorporates a digital technology[61].

This type of mentoring has always been useful, but never more so than now. Prior to the beginning of 2020, no one could have imagined that the whole world would have to live for a period in social isolation, and yet thanks to the Internet, we have been able to remain connected during this period. Unprecedented circumstances like this have demonstrated that the mentor's role is indispensable.

And the trend to acquire future skills through mentoring and work-based learning (WBL) will continue. E-mentoring can be very useful in getting digital capabilities into the workforce by creating bridges in LDBs between young learners with a high degree of digital literacy and their senior colleagues and instructors. Industry 4.0 therefore represents the future as it will allow companies to combine productivity and quickness in responding to the market. It is clear, though, that they need to invest in their staff competencies if they do not want to be excluded from the global competition[62]. In response to this, there is a growing trend in mentoring platforms and mobile apps, which offer free mentoring in a wide range of disciplines[63]. The question now is, will we witness the emergence of a robot mentor or coach in the near future? A 'botmentor' or a 'botcoach' that can answer all our questions and predict our moves, and intervene where needed. A dedicated private botmentor that lives with us 24/7 and can act like a consort? We will find out soon.

Mentoring in action

Case study: Mirage Aqua Park
Back at our case study at Mirage Aqua Park, it was noticeable that coaching and mentoring were being used interchangeably. What's more, there was no evidence of any formal initiative in relation to mentoring; managers and team leaders were simply perceived as mentors by the nature of their roles and personalities. The general manager in particular seemed to be viewed as a role model by all employees, as every respondent praised him and his management style. In this situation, the generation of information takes a one-way route as it flows from the senior managers, managers and team leaders to their subordinates (mentees). The communication and activities in this regard are thus limited to the concerned departments and business units. However, the fact that every manager is also a mentor is perceived by mentees as being important:

'I think it is a must for any manager or team leader to be a coach and a mentor. It is part of their job responsibility, and here you can see it during the course of every day. Our best mentor is the GM and also the park manager. We do not have assigned mentors as it depends on the individual themselves.' – Sarah, booking officer, Mirage Aqua Park

Similar to coaching, in this scenario, mentoring involves information being shared and integrated through one-to-one discussions, and not across the organization. Alternatively, it may be limited to the boundaries of the department or business unit. It was obvious that most of the mentoring activities at Mirage Aqua Park occurred during the newcomers' orientation period. Employees and managers were empowered to take appropriate actions and make their own decisions. This means that there is no identified route or special consideration for the mentoring practice. Instead, it is being carried out in a somewhat ad hoc manner.

Case study: LAMAR Hotels & Resorts

The management of LAMAR Hotels & Resorts realized that the local employees were reluctant to ask questions related to the job and that they also might require individualized training because of their different educational backgrounds. For this reason, they established a structured mentoring programme, which included an agreement between the mentor and the mentee. Each director and manager appoints a 'buddy' to new employees, who acts as a mentor; he or she answers the mentee's inquiries and helps him/her to become familiar with the system in a smooth manner.

In addition, as part of the scheme, information is generated by the mentors and, in many cases, by the mentees, in addition to the organization's literature and management system. Information is then communicated through a large number of internal communication channels, especially during brainstorming sessions and regular reviews.

This is fine in theory, yet it was evident that the programme was not as effective as the HR manager expected it would be, and it remained a challenge to convince the local employees to join the programme and utilize it effectively. This demonstrates clearly that culture plays a role in the mentoring relationship and often impacts its success.

'Some of my colleagues are shy and do not like to ask, as they do not want to be perceived as people who do not know something. In addition, their English language is not that good, and as you see, all the managers speak fluent English, so my colleagues are embarrassed to go and talk to them. They are, sometimes, worried that their managers will not appreciate it if they go and talk to other managers outside their department.

I think HR should redesign the programme in a better way.' – Amina, guest service officer, LAMAR Hotels & Resorts

This explanation for the scheme's lack of success was confirmed by another respondent, who also believed that many of the employees were shy and did not want to be perceived as being beginners or ignorant:

'We have a programme in place, but we are having a challenge with some colleagues who do not want to have a mentor. They seem to be either shy or do not want to be perceived as beginners who cannot work alone, so we are appointing a mentor (or in their view a teacher) for them. They think it is a sign of weakness.' – Badr, room service supervisor, LAMAR Hotels & Resorts

According to many employees, their manager should be their mentor, and there was some confusion about who could access the programme.

'I heard about the mentor programme, I do not know if it is only for local employees or anyone can participate. I think it is easier and faster to talk to my manager. For me, my mentor is my manager. Alternatively, I can go to the HR Department if there is a problem with my manager. Why should I go to someone else?' – Rasha, senior officer, sales, LAMAR Hotels & Resorts

Cultural issues clearly seem to have had an impact on the successful implementation of mentoring programmes in this case, e.g. mentees perceive themselves as being seen by others as lacking experience. They therefore had negative perceptions about being mentored. In the same vein, some managers were not keen to assign a mentor from other departments to 'their' team members – they considered that it affected their 'power', which in some cases created conflicts and clashes between the mentees and their managers.

This clash was evident at LAMAR Hotels & Resorts, where the mentoring scheme was structured and formalized into the system, whereas in Mirage Aqua Park there was no clash, since they did not feel the need to have a dedicated mentoring programme as it is already embedded into their work system and subsystems. Observations from both companies therefore confirm the need for the supportive relationship not only between the mentor and the mentee but also within the entire workplace.

What is coaching?

As defined by Eric Parsloe[64], coaching is 'a process that enables learning and development to occur and thus performance to improve'. Which is very generic and vague. The *Cambridge Dictionary*[65], meanwhile, defines coaching as 'the job or activity of providing training for people or helping to prepare them for something'. However, we believe that this definition isn't quite right in the context of business, because in business coaching is not training or preparation, in the same way as it would be in sport, for example[66] – instead it helps and supports a person on the way to achieving a business or career goal. Coaching should be understood, and managers should be trained to become better coaches since 'their degree of expertise and competence will have a great impact on the effectiveness of their coaching programmes'[67].

In a business sense, coaching is not merely a method for improving performance; rather, it is a mechanism that can be adopted by managers that includes, but is not limited to, job development, reward schemes, problem-solving, goal setting, compensation and training. Coaches are always behind the scenes. As in sporting games, they help coachees to achieve their targets, improve their skills – such as negotiation, selling, product design and management – and to diagnose what is going wrong. It's also important that managers understand the ways in which those whom they are coaching prefer to learn.

Bowerman and Collins[68] argue that the dialogue and conversation between coaches and learners can act as a vehicle to bring about both individual and organizational transformation. Conversation throughout coaching transfers implicit knowledge to explicit knowledge, which can then be translated into action. They state that coaching can have many forms and that the term 'coaching' is commonly used interchangeably with 'mentoring'. However, they are reluctant to give a definition for coaching because definitions can be limiting. To validate this approach, they argue that Reg Revans, the father of action learning, never provided a definition for action learning. However, they do go so far as to *distinguish* between mentoring and coaching. Mentoring has connotations with boss/subordinate relations on the one hand, while on the other hand, it is often associated with the new hires who are assigned an experienced staff member to ensure they are involved in the organization's system.

By contrast, we argue that it is important to provide a definition in order to classify knowledge and to help businesses recognize the most appropriate mechanisms for them. We see coaching as an approach that is based on people helping others to attain knowledge, skills and insights and to achieve desired outcomes in a democratic online and offline relationship. Coaching is a mechanism that management can use to improve performance because it helps managers to delegate tasks to their team members if the latter have been coached in how to handle the tasks. Moreover, a qualified coach is considered an enabler or learning connector within the LDB. Coaching can help foster employee empowerment and contribute to making the individual learning organizational, and vice versa. Coaching can cut across the hierarchies and boundaries of the LDB; managers can act as coaches to their subordinates and employees can act as coaches to their peers in other business units. Whenever a manager performs a task that someone else can do, they prevent themselves from performing a task that only they can do. When delegating, the managers who act like coaches will not select the ready employees who can do the job. Rather, they will choose the employees who do not yet have the skills to do the job. The manager therefore acts as a coach by helping that employee to attain the required skill and by sharing their knowledge.

Coaching in action: West Yorkshire Police

In the UK, since 2010, many public sector organizations have experienced severe cuts to their budgets as part of austerity policies implemented by government. This has had an impact on staff attitudes. One such organization is West Yorkshire Police (WYP), an organization that employs 8,000 staff. In 2014, the chief officer commissioned a survey of staff opinions that indicated that leader engagement with staff was poor at all levels, with low levels of trust and a perceived lack of visible support for change from leaders. As part of a broader initiative to address such issues, leaders were invited to participate in a coaching programme designed to allow leaders to become aware of patterns of working and to make the leaders more visible.

At WYP, 10 leaders agreed to participate in the coaching programme. To provide them with key skills and a learning process, a framework based on narrative coaching was employed[69]. This approach is based on a view of people, as natural storytellers, using stories as a means of communicating with each other – for good or ill. If, through interaction, leaders can adopt a narrative coaching position, they can allow a space for others to tell stories of their experiences. By listening carefully, they can catch a glimpse of what is happening and can respond. They can also step back and reflect on the key features, which can then be shared with other leaders to improve their business. In this way, coaching can link to organizational learning. The coaches at WYP agreed to complete learning logs of their interactions and meet in an action learning group of five people every four weeks for a period of three months.

The process was soon recognized as a way for leaders to become more visible to their staff, and it was discovered that the staff were found to be 'more accepting of the fact that change is here and it is happening now'. Leaders also found 'simple and obvious' actions that required close engagement to provide the clarity that was needed. For example, the process enabled the dispelling of a myth that had been allowed to flourish – that one section would be closed down. The box below shows an example of a learning log, completed following a coaching conversation.

A log completed after coaching

'I travelled to outer-lying offices (B & T). As well as reaffirming belief in the dedication of our staff (you'll see therefore that there's as much benefit for me as there was to them!), there was a distinctive theme here: that staff at the smaller offices felt a greater sense of togetherness than those at the regional office at H. That's not to say that the spirit at H is not good, because I think it is, certainly compared to other offices I've worked at. It did make me conscious that with a bit of diary planning, I could do this far more often than I do and the value is in just simply talking without having to make any massive promises on how the world will get better overnight.'

In each case, by summarizing the 'main points', participants revealed what they were learning from the conversations and these were taken to a review meeting, where themes were identified and possible actions considered. As the process continued, important issues relating to change, the pace of change, the settling of change and a silo mentality (where staff are reluctant to share information with others) were identified. A key issue was the importance of identity and the pride in how staff responded to challenge through the 'work they undertake' and the 'team ethos' they had created, and the crucial importance of 'effective collaboration...which is not always evident'. Pride was related to staff commitment to 'do my utmost to provide good service', 'do what it takes to meet my objectives' and 'go the "extra mile" to assist their customers'. One leader could conclude that 'people are worth the investment whatever their plans' and another concluded that:

> 'The obvious commitment and pride that this supervisor had in her work and the belief in the purpose of the work...was apparent from the outset. She was passionate in the belief that vulnerable victims had to be protected.'

The coaching leaders found that people were 'prepared to talk openly with senior staff, without intimidation' and demonstrated 'pride in serving their local community, even when there are problems and issues'. One clear finding related to communication, in particular reliance on emails; the coaches, by contrast, could respond within a face-to-face relationship, and this was deemed beneficial. For example, one leader reflected on the benefits of:

> '...just taking the time to speak for 20 minutes rather than rushing to my next meeting or set of emails. This does contrast with a previous conversation with staff who expressed doubts about their long-term future with the organization due to the possibility of further budget cuts...'

At the end of the process, there was a commitment to adopt the role of coaching leader and to contribute to the development of a learning culture even as austerity measures continued. Further, coaching had contributed to an improvement in the culture of WYP[70].

Summary

There is a great deal of overlap between coaching and mentoring in literature. In the LDB, and particularly in the emerging patterns of working in the post-Covid-19 era, we argue that leaders need to be visible and interact on a face-to-face basis, even if this is necessarily mediated by technology. Mentoring and coaching are key skills that enable leaders to provide 'social accountability' through a close and regular relationship with their staff[71]. In the LDB, it is important that the image of leader as coach becomes prevalent in order to promote a learning culture[72]. We believe that coaching can be practised in day-to-day activities, and is an enabler of the LDB, even if such activities are more dispersed during the post-Covid-19 era. This also applies to mentoring, which can occur at virtually any time and in any location[73].

4

Employees' Cross-Training

'While cross-training is popular in sports and a
great way of developing fitness, there is another type of
cross-training that has become popular in business
that is beneficial to the fitness and overall health of
both companies and employees.'
John Yurkschatt[74]

Introduction

As we undertake research or assess or advise companies and
help them transform into a Learning-Driven Business, we
often come across methods and techniques that prove to be
very useful and leverage performance. We have observed
that when there is curiosity about the task and when it is
employee-driven, there are often excellent outputs. One of
the practices that we investigated and witnessed is 'cross-
training' (CRT), which is intensively adopted in specific
sectors such as healthcare, banking, hospitality, insurance,
retail and manufacturing. In this chapter, we will answer

the questions about what, how and why CRT can help the LDB to transform and to sustain learning. Considering the pressing need for career shifts and the acquisition of new skills and competences in the Industry 4.0/machine learning era (see Chapter 9) and post-Covid-19, we argue that CRT will receive much more attention and will become a remit for almost every LDB.

What is cross-training?

As defined by Laura Williams[75], the fitness expert, cross-training is 'any workout that complements routine, helping to even out potential muscle imbalances or weaknesses. It ultimately enhances fitness levels while reducing the likelihood of injury'. Julia Baverstock[76], a well-being personal trainer, explains that CRT adds different types of training into a routine to achieve a more rounded set of skills that the body can call on when needed – for example, adding occasional running or swimming to a cyclist's training plan. This works different muscle groups and requires the body to adapt, and therefore to get stronger and fitter because it is being challenged to do something it is not used to. Furthermore, CRT adds variety, which helps people stay motivated and engaged, and it also raises the metabolism because the body is adapting to the different muscles being worked. Behind the scenes, the neuromuscular changes that occur in response to the challenges of CRT create different muscle and connective tissue adaptations, which enhance movement and flexibility. So, as you can see, it is beneficial in a sports context on many different levels.

The same is true in the world of business, a context in which the phrase is a relative newcomer. Its application and definition remains valid here because LDBs are expected to learn and draw from various disciplines in order to grow stronger and improve. There should be osmosis across skill sets whenever relevant. This is almost exactly what happens in employee cross-training. For example, an employee working as a teller in a bank can engage in cross-training as a credit officer in the Operations Department. In this way, he/she can learn new practices and understand the processes at the other end. Not only this, but the employee can become qualified to assume a different role when needed. This mechanism therefore helps employees to enhance their skill set and employability and also improve the internal communication and synergy within the bank.

In order to explore this further, we consulted databases to identify documented literature on this mechanism. We came across professional and industry publications rather than academic research, suggesting that although the practice (albeit not necessarily called 'cross-training') is not new, it is under-investigated. So, for clarity, we propose the following definition:

> Cross-training is an on-job training mechanism that is meant to improve performance and continuous learning, whereby employees engage with the acquisition of new skills and knowledge from a different business area within their organization to widen their horizons and enhance individual, team and organizational performance.

Cross-training also encompasses other OL mechanisms, such as mentoring, coaching and dialogue (see Figure 4.1)

In the LDB, leaders and learning and development professionals should think of CRT as a disaster recovery plan. If CRT is implemented correctly, it could help the business to run smoothly in the event that one or more team member is absent[77]. On the other hand, employees could think of CRT as a way to develop employable skills by learning new things and socializing with colleagues at other business units, becoming more valuable to the company and enhancing their contribution to the company.

FIGURE 4.1   Combinable Elements of Cross-training

Source: Developed by the authors

Who in a business should be cross-trained? Abrams and Berge[78] stated that it depends on a few factors, such as the purpose of CRT, the cost of training, the need to make changes in workflow, the need to preserve task specialization in some areas and, most importantly, employees' willingness to be cross-trained and perform multiple tasks. As we argue in Chapter 9, with many businesses adopting machine learning and artificial intelligence technologies, non-data science professionals such as HR, marketing and accounting professionals need to cross-train in order to become hybrid professionals who can exert an influence on such projects. Further, during the initial phases of the Covid-19 era, when illness or home duties meant some staff could not work, CRT was advocated in order to provide flexibility[79]. As uncertainty continues to affect where and how people work and learn, the LDB needs to plan for CRT to offer provision that functions across different channels[80].

In the two businesses that we investigated, the CRT process starts with self-nomination, i.e. with an employee who is willing to be cross-trained, but this step comes after the business units providing cross-training have advertised a vacancy for CRT. For example, when there is a need for trainees in an Operations Department, they liaise with the HR Department to promote the vacancy, and then employees from other departments can apply. The need for the cross-trainee stems from a potential job vacancy or lack of manpower, and the proposed scheme requires work contributions from the cross-trainees to ameliorate the situation.

Why does a LDB adopt CRT?

Salim and Abdien[81] investigated the impacts of cross-training on job performance, employee retention and service quality as being critical indicators in the hospitality sector. They surveyed 427 employees and, among several findings, they concluded that cross-trained employees proved to have better task performance practices than those who had not been cross-trained, including demonstrating expertise in all job-related tasks, managing more responsibility than had been typically assigned, and performing well in the overall job by carrying out tasks precisely as expected. There was also a positive correlation between CRT and employee retention as employees become more proud to be part of their organization, more committed to their jobs and more interested in their tasks. Besides, cross-trained employees exhibited the ability to improve service quality by supporting teamwork both inside and outside their departments. This increased their ability to solve problems and promptly discover potential service defects. They were ready to offer excellent service right from the word go, and utilized their acquired knowledge from CRT to provide prompt solutions to customer complaints and service quality-related problems.

Stanica and Peydro[82] consider CRT to be a lean tool. Lean thinking aims to organize human activities to eliminate waste and create value for individuals[83]. CRT as a lean tool involves interaction and learning among people and hence involves knowledge transfer. We argue that businesses agree that the implementation of cross-training will have a positive effect on this knowledge transfer processes. Other significant advantages that are detected are that cross-training broadens the knowledge and the competences of employees, and that it helps the business to manage the tacit knowledge. However, there are some drawbacks, such as the lack of metrics for measuring the knowledge transfer, low speed of knowledge transfer and potential restriction to creativity in cases where the knowledge sharer insists on doing things in one particular way without providing opportunities to the knowledge receiver (i.e. the cross-trainee) to change or develop these. Nevertheless, cross-training can improve the learning curve organization-wide and facilitate knowledge transfer smoothly and in a cost-effective manner. Below, we list some of the perceived benefits of CRT at work. Cross-training:

1 helps employee to diversify their knowledge and experience, resulting in greater satisfaction;
2 breaks the daily routine and provides new insights on how employees see their job;

3 improves work relations, as cross-teams are expected to further understand what other colleagues are doing in other job roles;

4 means that employees can cover for their colleagues in case of absence or when needed;

5 creates more opportunities for employees to change their job roles internally;

6 enhances employability in case of redundancy or desire of employees to seek further career growth;

7 is cost-effective, as the LDB does not need to hire trainers or buy training packages; the only investment is employees' time;

8 means that employees learn from the best as the provider of the training will be someone who is a practitioner and knows their job better than anyone else;

9 motivates employees and increases their retention;

10 provides a significant boost to the workforce's productivity and the bottom line[84];

11 contributes to creating further career paths for employees;

12 provides an opportunity for discovering new talents and especially new leaders;

13 reduces the cost of external recruiting as it helps HR to have a pool of qualified internal employees who know the business.

CRT is one of the most effective methods of improving both the individual employee's and team performance. However, whether or not CRT is advantageous or disadvantageous depends on how it is implemented; organizational culture needs to be considered in order to maximize the benefits. For example, employees can be cross-trained in different departments but within their skill domain. CRT mechanism can be used in many positions in many sectors. For example, businesses whose representatives have intensive customer interactions could cross-train their service staff in a variety of roles to ensure empathy with the customer – i.e. retail businesses could cross-train cashiers and customer service staff. Technology-focused businesses, to take a different example, may prefer that their employees should gain knowledge of the entire portfolio of offerings and to this end attract the individuals who invest time and energy in broadening their knowledge with bonuses and other benefits.

Asselta and Sperl[85] consider CRT as a win-win approach. As employees' values and needs are changing, so are those of organizations. Cross-training is an effective method that may be used to align the values and needs of both the employees and the organization. Today's employers are looking for versatile and flexible workers. They want team players willing to accept or even volunteer for tasks or projects beyond their usual duties. The last thing they want to hear is 'that's not my job' or 'I don't know how to do it.' According to Asselta and Sperl, though, cross-training is not for every organization since there are impediments and costs associated with its implementation. The barriers can be internal or external and involve both organizational and individual issues. For instance, CRT is not suitable for start-ups at the beginning of the growth cycle as the focus would be on meeting immediate needs. However, towards the end of the growth cycle, CRT may be useful to re-energize the business.

Cross-training in action: LAMAR Hotels & Resorts

During our observations at LAMAR Hotels & Resorts, we came across the following definition in their training manual[86]:

'Cross Training is training in a job other than the trainee's current job. This can be in the same department or a different department in the same business unit or a different business unit. There is no distinction between training undertaken in your department or a different department.'

The manual also explains why employees should consider it:

'Cross Training allows you to work with colleagues who possess specialized expertise to which you might otherwise not have access. This will place you in a position to make more informed decisions about alternative careers in our exciting industry. Please note that while Cross Training allows you to prepare for a possible future career move, it does not automatically mean that you will be guaranteed a job in the area where you are training.'

The implementation of cross-training appeared to be very structured and known to everyone in the organization. The proportion of employees who had completed cross-training was high. It was found that the organization had benefited from this approach in terms of internal promotion and recruitment. Furthermore, the newly acquired skills were implemented by cross-trainees. In this practice, there is a two-way learning highway; on the one hand, information is generated and shared by the trainer from the host department, and on the other hand, the trainee shares information about his/her department and the way they do business, which enriches both parties.

In terms of logistics, both parties agree on a plan, and the whole cross-training exercise has to be executed within a maximum of three months in order to allow other trainees to undertake such training. Since the launch of the cross-training programme in 2002, more than 1,000 employees have completed their cross-training (60 hours). In terms of the benefits, promotion and availability of CRT vacancies, it is highly visible and promoted across the organization.

New information travels across departments and, where training takes place within the one department, information travels across sections within this department. The benefits have two dimensions:

1 Short-term benefits, at the level of concerned employees involved in the programme;
2 Long-term benefits when these employees get back to their departments/business units to share the experience and knowledge with their colleagues or reflect on what they have learned and experiment with new ways of doing what they used to do.

Decisions about cross-training-related activities are left to the employees. Almost all employees were found to be keen on this practice, e.g. trainees were eager to enhance and diversify their set of skills, while the managers/ hosts were interested in getting free support. Cross-training is also part of the quality management system. There are documented procedures and guidelines that explain it.

It seems that cross-training had certain side benefits and a positive impact on other approaches, as explained by a respondent who attributed the success of teamwork to cross-training:

1. Task trainers: the organization identified individual employees who were considered to be experts in their

fields (e.g. chefs, butchers, waiters or housekeepers) as 'task trainers', their expertise being utilized to train recruits or to enhance the skills of other employees as a training intervention and an ongoing coaching process.

2. Departmental trainers: these are qualified trainers who have attended a 'Train the Trainer' course, comprising activities including the following:

1 Delivery of formal training, e.g. guest service modules;
2 Delivery of on-the-job training, e.g. coaching on operational skills;
3 Conducting training in weekly activities;
4 Delivering training when a new procedure, technique or piece of information is taught;
5 Providing training when a procedure, technique or piece of information is revised.

Both types of trainers continue to pursue their primary job, i.e. they are not full-time trainers. The critical difference between them is that departmental trainers are qualified trainers who have attended a course and met individual formal requirements so that they can conduct group courses. Task trainers, by contrast, are not qualified trainers, but rather coaches for specific tasks in which they are considered experts. The Training Department asks these people to train recruits in one-to-one sessions, in addition to working with existing staff who need skill enhancement.

The skills newly acquired by the trainees in the case of LAMAR Hotels & Resorts were utilized well. For example, an employee was seconded to ensure the safety of a visiting VIP female guest after having completed her cross-training in the security department, despite the fact that her main job was not related to security. The senior management therefore recognized this employee for her professionalism and made good use of her skills.

'I think one of the reasons for successful teamwork here is the cross-training because we build relations with colleagues in other departments when we go there. They also come to our department, and we exchange knowledge, experience, learn how to solve different problems and have some sort of professional friendship and rapport within the workplace.' – Fernanda, receptionist, LAMAR Hotels & Resorts

Individual Development Plans (IDPs)
There was evidence that LAMAR Hotels & Resorts has established many initiatives to encourage employees to attain further education and enhance their skill sets. Respondent B24, for instance, was undertaking a course to obtain a professional qualification from the CIPD and pursuing an assignment on the benchmarking of

individual development plans (IDPs) that required her to interact with two organizations outside the hospitality field in order to learn how they designed and implemented their IDPs.

Employees whom we observed appraised the cross-training scheme and appreciated its role. Furthermore, data shows exponential growth and a positive trend in the number of individuals who joined the scheme.

Summary

As we have seen during the Covid-19 pandemic, doctors and other health professionals – as well as many other professionals across multiple sectors – have to quickly cross-train to learn the skills required to cope with a crisis[87]. We believe that further responses to and developments in machine learning will result in the increased use of CRT. While there are not yet many documented studies that can reveal the impacts of CRT or highlight various methods of implementation, we would encourage readers to share their experience with us[88]. It should be noted that although there have been many studies on 'job rotation', CRT differs from this since it does not merely involve the rotation of employees. CRT is not intended to teach new 'jobs' but to be a channel for learning new tasks or aspects of jobs in another business function, within the same company or a sister company. CRT can be a very useful and effective mechanism as it fosters internal promotions, the retainment of individuals and disseminates knowledge and learning across the LDB. CRT can act as a vehicle for career improvement and growth and for exercising and learning new skill sets that could benefit employees in their current assignment or when they move to other organizations.

Part Two

WHY TEAM
LEARNING?

- ✦ Chapter 5: After-action Reviews (AARs)
- ✦ Chapter 6: Problem-solving Teams (PSTs)
- ✦ Chapter 7: Action Learning Sets (Learning Circles) (ALS)
- ✦ Chapter 8: Futures and Foresight Learning

'Team learning is vital because teams, not individuals, are the fundamental learning unit in modern organizations. This is where "the rubber meets the road"; unless teams can learn, the organization cannot learn.' – Peter M. Senge in *The Fifth Discipline*[89]

One of the pillars of organizational learning, as described in the LDO model[90], is group/team learning (GTL) and by that we mean the learning that occurs within a group or team setting. Group/Team Learning (GTL) can act as the middle cogs in a trilogy of learning (see Figure B1), because it is an ideal bridge between individual learning and organization-wide learning. Teams are a collection of individuals who are interdependently working to achieve a shared goal[91] and organizations have come to rely on teams that can learn to be successful[92]. Indeed, one of the most crucial functions teams perform for these organizations is learning.

When teams do not learn, the organization will likely suffer. For example, teams that fail to learn will take longer to bring a new product to market[93]. Hence, it has become crucial in both practice and academia to

FIGURE B1   Trilogy of Learning within the Learning-Driven Business (LDB)

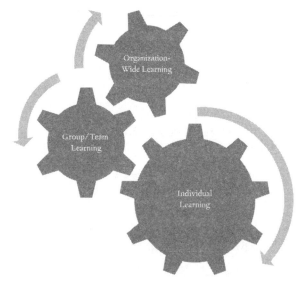

better understand team learning to enhance effectiveness throughout organizations. For this reason, it is crucial that researchers and practitioners alike take the time and effort to understand teams better.

Amy Edmondson[94] defines team learning as an ongoing behavioural process – representing the cyclical process of seeking out feedback, gathering questions and discussing and integrating information. Over the years, the research on team learning has evolved, having looked at various types of team learning behaviours, which is used to encapsulate all of the actions that aid in the development of collective knowledge. These actions, however, are not qualitatively similar. Wiese and Burke[95] break them down into three different types: 1. intrateam; 2. interteam; 3. fundamental learning behaviours.

1 Intrateam learning behaviours

These reflect the internal processes teams engage in to build shared meaning from existing information, identify and fill in gaps in the team's collective knowledge, and challenge, test, and explore assumptions. Asking questions, experimenting, discussing errors and outcomes, constructive criticism and exploration are some examples of these behaviours. Intrateam learning behaviours reflect how the team obtains information from their fellow team members and how that information is integrated into their collective knowledge; they do not necessarily reflect the actions of sharing information with the team. In other words, they are the knowledge-obtaining and scaffolding processes that occur within the immediate team.

2 Interteam learning behaviours

These behaviours occur when teams seek and integrate information from individuals outside the immediate team. Some of these behaviours include asking questions and seeking feedback. Individuals outside the team are likely to bring new and different perspectives to the team's dynamic compared to those offered by internal team members[96].

3 Fundamental learning behaviours

These behaviours represent the basic learning processes that promote learning in teams[97]. Unlike intrateam and interteam learning behaviours, fundamental learning behaviours are actions that individual team members take to share, store and retrieve information. Wiese and Burke argue that sharing represents the actions teams take to make their fellow members aware of individually held information. Fundamental behaviours exclusively represent how knowledge is transported across time. While sharing represents how knowledge is transported from the individual to the team, storage behaviours illustrate how collective knowledge is preserved across time. Similarly, retrieval processes are those that represent how collective knowledge is transferred from repositories to the team's awareness.

In this part, Chapter 5 discusses the critical role of the after-action review and how it works as a mechanism for team learning. Chapter 6 covers problem-solving and how a dedicated team for problem-solving may enrich learning and improvement. Chapter 7 discusses action learning sets, which are a significant component of action learning, and we end with Chapter 8, which addresses futures and foresight learning.

5

After-action Reviews (AARs)

'The Army's After Action Review (AAR) is arguably
one of the most successful organizational learning
methods yet devised. Yet, most every corporate
effort to graft this truly innovative practice into their
culture has failed because, again and again, people reduce
the living practice of AARs to a sterile technique.'
Peter Senge, MIT-based author, researcher & educator[98]

Introduction

In late August 2005, Hurricane Katrina struck the south-
eastern US. The hurricane and its aftermath claimed more
than 1,800 lives, and it ranked as the costliest natural
disaster in US history[99]. After the hurricane, the Centers for
Disease Control and Prevention (CDC) formed an after-
action review workgroup to conduct an aftermath exercise.
The AAR workgroup was asked to identify strengths and
areas for improvement in CDC's hazard preparedness and
response investment so they could improve organizational

performance and save people's lives. A series of extended interviews were duly conducted with staff members, the Federal Emergency Management Agency, many public and private agencies, and international organizations such as the World Health Organization. Policies, processes and procedures were carefully reviewed and mapped against CDC's emergency response activities. Vast amounts of data and information were analysed, and the outcome of the AAR was a 223-page report[100]. This exercise led to new systems for communications during natural disasters. One team member reported, 'Without an AAR you keep learning your lessons again the hard way!'[101]

Such an example is typical of an AAR mechanism, which usually takes the form of a facilitated discussion following an event or activity. It enables understanding of the expectations and perspectives of team members involved in capturing learning and extracting learned lessons, which can then be shared more widely and become organizational. As such, it is one of the most substantial and robust mechanisms for making the team and group learning organizational.

What are AARs and why do they exist?

All sorts of businesses exist to cater for their customers. To meet performance standards, it is imperative that employees and their leaders understand whether their daily operations contribute to the organization's mission. This is valuable for all employees because they get the opportunity to learn collectively from each other's successes and failures. Front-line employees who interact with customers daily or work on the shop floor are often the best people to provide input on how the business can achieve maximum value from its operations. Such inputs are a prime source of emergent learning for strategy. For organizational learning to occur, there are various mechanisms and activities that organizations can optimize, one of which is AARs.

The AAR was originally conceptualized by the US Army and continues to be used by military organizations worldwide to provide candid feedback on group performance in training and combat. After-action review is defined as: 'A simple instrument which helps project team members to learn after any team task or event. It brings together relevant team members and allows them to evaluate the outcomes of their actions and draw lessons for the future'[102]. In simple terms, an AAR is the professional discussion of a specific event that has occurred. It helps participants discover for themselves what happened, why it happened, and how to sustain strengths and improve weaknesses in performance. Participants investigate a situation, use problem-solving to identify strengths and weaknesses, propose solutions and adopt a course of action to ensure effective behaviour in the future. In this sense, the AAR is similar to problem-solving. The difference is that an AAR takes place after the event; it cannot occur before or during the event, unless it tackles a long-term problem.

In addition, an AAR is not dependent on problems or incidents having occurred; it takes place regardless of what happened. AARs are offline, internal, formal and reactive; *internal* practice because they are executed by the individuals who were involved in the event, and *reactive* because they occur only after the event is over[103].

In the US Army's 'Leader Guide to AARs'[104], there is specific emphasis on the spirit with which AARs are conducted. The environment of an AAR should be one where employees and their managers are comfortable to honestly discuss an event in sufficient detail so that everyone understands what occurred and why. More importantly, participants should have a strong desire to seek the opportunity to practice the task again. Active participation by all employees is essential in making an AAR a success. Leaders determine who the right participants are for the AAR. In some cases, having a larger number of participants may lead to better results. In other cases, such as strategic discussions, only key participants may be invited. Discussing the event may provide insights that are not normally recorded in the operating procedures, and that in itself could be a collective learning opportunity. AARs typically have four phases and these are summarized in Table 5.1

The range of topics addressed in an AAR can vary widely. It can be used to discuss events related to planning, performance, attitude, communication, safety, responsibilities, techniques or lessons learned. Whatever the

TABLE 5.1 *AAR's Four-step Cycle*[105]

Step	Actions
Planning	✦ Schedule the AAR ✦ Select an AAR facilitator (optional) ✦ Establish the AAR agenda and select location ✦ Notify participants ✦ Assemble AAR materials (designs, codes etc.)
Preparation	✦ Review the expected outcomes for the project or event ✦ Prepare the AAR site ✦ Identify key events to discuss
Conduct	✦ Seek maximum participation ✦ Maintain focus on AAR objectives ✦ Review key lessons learned ✦ Record the AAR
Follow-up	✦ Distribute a record of the AAR to all participants ✦ Publish lessons learned in an easily accessible location ✦ Prioritize actions ✦ Develop an action plan to fix the problem (revise SOPs, develop a new process etc.)

subject, fundamentally, participants discuss the following questions related to an incident:

1 What was planned?
2 What really happened?
3 Why did it happen?
4 What are the implications of what happened?
5 What can we do better next time?

Research indicates that the AAR practice brings many benefits to an organization because it promotes continuous improvement by learning from experience[106] and applying its results to future situations. And, after all, that is the essence of business excellence. The practice of AAR, as discussed in this chapter, is simple to use and may be implemented in any business situation. Table 5.2 gives a summary of the dos and don'ts of a successful AAR[107].

TABLE 5.2 *Summary of Dos and Don'ts of AAR*

Dos	*Don'ts*
Schedule AARs shortly after the completion of an activity Make reviews routine	Conduct AARs without planning Schedule reviews irregularly
Collect objective data whenever possible	Allow debates to bog down discussions when identifying facts
Use trained facilitators	Allow dominating leaders to run AARs
Establish clear ground rules ✦ Encourage candour ✦ Focus on the incident and not on the person reporting it ✦ Determine what can be fixed immediately ✦ Keep discussions confidential	Base performance evaluations or promotions on mistakes admitted in AARs
Proceed systematically ✦ What did we set out to do? ✦ What actually happened? ✦ Why did it happen? ✦ What are we going to do next time?	Permit unstructured, meandering discussion
Involve all participants	Allow senior managers or facilitators to dominate discussions
Probe for underlying cause-and-effect relationships	Criticize individual behaviour or performance
Identify activities to be sustained as well as errors to be avoided	Conclude without a list of actions to be applied in the future

AARs and other learning mechanisms

As we've discussed, an AAR is an offline, internal, formal and reactive process that encourages reflection and brainstorming. However, both Mirage Aqua Park and LAMAR Hotels & Resorts have complemented and strengthened their AAR protocol with *follow-up*. This means that the outcome of this practice is subject to audit on a regular basis to ensure the implementation of the agreed action, including changes in the operation manuals, standard operating procedures (SOPs) and policies. The main reason Mirage Aqua Park and LAMAR Hotels & Resorts rely on AARs stems from their working environments. Since both firms provide hospitality services, they have an urgent need to fix errors and implement appropriate measures for issues related to guests' health and safety, such as slides and rides at Mirage Aqua Park. Awareness of these matters can be organization wide; we clearly noticed a shift from IL (individual learning) to GL (group learning) taking place during these AAR meetings in various departments. It should be noted, however, that while AAR is an excellent method to glean insights into daily operations, it is not the cure-all for organizational issues. Front-line employees and their managers should own specific tasks within the business and modify them as the situation demands, sometimes even before they have had an opportunity to discuss them with the larger group. Nevertheless, AAR remains a valuable and widely used learning tool that supports performance excellence. When conducted in the right spirit, it enhances individual and team performance. The result is a more cohesive organization.

More than a meeting or a post-mortem

AARs can be used by organizations of any size and from any sector. However, they should not be considered as a mere meeting to document lessons learned; they should be used in a way that treats every interaction or incident as an opportunity for learning about what to do and how to think and act. Marilyn Darling and her colleagues[108] analysed a vast number of AARs and lessons learned processes at more than a dozen corporations, non-profit organizations and government agencies in order to understand why some organizations still do not learn despite conducting AARs. They found out that the fundamentals were the same at all organizations they visited, i.e. following a project or event, team members gather to share insights and identify errors. Although the businesses they studied actively looked for lessons, few learned them in a meaningful way, and they repeated the same mistakes simply because the focus deviated from the action and was geared towards the review. The conclusion is that AAR is not just the meeting or the post-mortem, it is meant to be a live mechanism for *action* rather than formalities and documentations. Without action, AAR will not add any value, and it will lose its purpose. The lesson learned here is simple and can be summarized in one tiny word: ACT!

A second success factor is that AARs have to be held periodically but consistently and after every activity or project. This is in line with the dynamics of certain types of business more than others; for example, hotels run the AAR with every shift change and every morning, and some airlines run it after each flight. It is also a widespread practice in hospitals. The UK National Health Service (NHS) uses it frequently, for example, and it is an effective mechanism for continuous improvement and learning that has been embedded in their knowledge mobilization framework (KMF) (Figure 5.1). In fact, so great is the value they place on it that the NHS offers free e-learning training on AAR[109].

Although the traditional form of an AAR is after the event, as suggested in Figure 5.1, AARs can also be used while the project is progressing. Instead of waiting until the end of a long project to evaluate performance; hence it is conducted after completion of each phase or stage, which

FIGURE 5.1 NHS Knowledge Mobilization Framework, Including AAR

Learning Before	Learning During	Learning After
Self Assessment Tool	After-Action Reviews	Knowledge Harvesting
Peer Assist	Knowledge Cafe	Retrospect
Before Action Review	Randomised Coffee Trials	
	Communities of Practice	
	Action Learning Sets	
	Knowledge Assets	

Knowledge Mobilisation for Health Organisations

Source: Courtesy of eLearning for Healthcare, NHS

we call In-Action Reviews or (IARs). IARs incorporate continuous learning right from the start and provide an effective and easy-to-use mechanism for capturing lessons learned from activities and projects. What's more, if used effectively, IARs can be great for ensuring that the lessons learned from one project or team are shared organization wide, to improve overall performance.

You can see, then, that AARs help us keep open a steady dialogue about organizational learning and continuous improvement. They also allow organizations to learn and adapt so that they can keep up with – and stay ahead of – change[110]. In addition, working with critical thinking and the reflection ideas we considered in Chapters 1 and 2, AARs can surface and challenge underlying assumptions.

EFQM[111] defined AARs as a 'simple instrument that help[s] project team members to evaluate the outcome of their actions and draw lessons for future', so the learning in this context starts at an individual level, whereby 'individuals meet and reflect on what has happened, they discuss and share ideas, they explain to each other so everyone [can] realize and further form his/her own picture, then together they try to match the actual outcome to the expected outcome.' This mismatch is a key component here in terms of drawing lessons or actionable points that may lead to simple 'quick fix' actions, i.e. adaptive learning[112] or single-loop learning. It is believed that simple and daily routine actions will not leave the domain of adaptive learning unless there is a repeated issue – 'if it happens again...'

scenarios. This means that reoccurrence is a crucial element that necessitates further and deeper actions or questioning of assumptions, which may in turn lead to a review of the existing policies and approach to running the business.

A shift from individual learning to group learning and from group learning to organization-wide learning is expected to take place while practising AARs. Taking the learned lessons to the organizational level seems to be dependent on the criticality of the issue and how strategic it is. It is also dependent on procedural issues because someone or some function is expected to follow up on the agreed-upon actions.

After-action reviews in practice

During a series of live AARs conducted at both Mirage Aqua Park and the LAMAR Hotels & Resorts, it was observed that Mirage Aqua Park conducts informal AARs almost every single day. More formal AARs are conducted on a weekly, monthly and quarterly basis. The water park established a dedicated committee for assessment and review based on feedback received during a previous quality award assessment. This committee conducts a formal monthly review. During these reviews, participants examine specific incidents, and brainstorm and provide insight from their point of view on how these incidents arose. A wide range of issues is discussed, which deviates from the standard format of AAR as conducted by the US

Army. The format of AAR at Mirage is therefore a hybrid of AAR, problem-solving teams and action learning sets. This demonstrates that there is no one-size-fits-all approach using these mechanisms.

The USAID (United States Agency for International Development) practices AAR heavily, and it is embedded in its development projects. According to the USAID approach,[113] After-Action Reviews (AARs) and In-Action Reviews (IARs) play a role in redefining the goals or future targets. During implementation, the USAID team reviews the tasks and goals of the activity as they were initially understood. The team then evaluates whether these tasks and goals were effective after implementing the activity. Hence, the AAR also identifies any next steps or action items towards meeting these goals after the activity itself has finished. It is not a critique; in fact it has several advantages over a critique, for example:

1 It does not judge success or failure;
2 It attempts to discover why things happened;
3 It focuses directly on the tasks and goals that were to be accomplished;
4 It encourages team members to surface important lessons in the discussion;
5 More team members participate so that more of the project or activity can be recalled and more lessons can be learned, shared, and incorporated back into the project or subsequent projects.

'We discuss several matters like managing absence, performance issues and changes in the labour law. Whenever there is a change in the regulations, we sit together as an HR team and discuss our preparation for this. We do not let things go; we discuss everything in these meetings. Anything, for example if a guest abuses a colleague, we discuss it, and we try to find a good way to tackle these things.' – Rosana, HR director, Mirage Aqua Park

In case of amendments to policies or procedures, changes are approved by the business excellence director and relevant information is shared to all employees via briefing meetings, the Intranet, newsletters and several other channels. A summary of unsatisfactory incidents is documented department-wide under the heading 'Lessons Learned'. As information is shared throughout the organization, all employees can access it. They can also suggest new methods or use documented methods while tackling similar issues. AAR meetings are considered a means of collective interpretation of information since the members of the committees are representatives of all departments across the organization.

'Every month we have the assessment and review committee meeting – the members are about 20, and they voluntarily participate in the committee.' – Adam, member, assessment and review committee, Mirage Aqua Park

During these meetings, the focus is on *action*; once something has been agreed upon, everyone understands their responsibilities and initiates immediate action. Employees are conscious about learning on the job as they perform their new tasks. They also have clear directions on performance standards, and there is a transparent employee rewards system. It's easy to spot both loops of learning here, although there is a greater focus on single-loop learning.

> 'We introduced [a] massage service based on a suggestion from a colleague. But we realized that it did not work, we did not receive requests from guests for this service although we promoted it well. To understand why this did not work as we expected, we formed an after-action review team to find out why. The team concluded that our service is expensive compared to similar services in the city, that's why people do not want to pay more here. They also determined that mornings may not be the right time for massage; it may be better to schedule these in the afternoon. We also asked our guests about this and listened to their feedback. Now we are going to reintroduce this service after we improve it based on the review we made.' – Angela, customer service team leader, Mirage Aqua Park

At LAMAR Hotels & Resorts, there are formal and informal AARs. The most frequent one occurs twice a day, at the beginning and end of employee shifts. The meeting typically tackles operational issues. For more strategic matters, formal brainstorming sessions and SWOT analysis are conducted. Information for AAR is generated during the meetings or as the outcome of surveys, audits, self-assessment or external assessment, such as the National Quality Award. LAMAR Hotels & Resorts has won many awards. Along with each award, the hotel receives a report that highlights both strengths and areas for improvement. Meetings and one-to-one informal discussions are the main ways that lessons learned are identified. The Learning and Development Department plays a major role in the organization and their contribution to performance improvement is appreciated by all employees. Information is shared with everyone, even if it is not directly related to their job. There is continuous and open dialogue among employees, vertically and horizontally; this organization uses its Intranet extensively to disseminate new information and lessons learned. The Learning and Development Department summarizes lessons, incidents and new issues in a weekly newsletter distributed to all employees by email and posted on the Intranet. As a consequence, employees and senior managers at LAMAR Hotels & Resorts are open to the implementation of new practices and actively question the logic and reasoning behind existing practices. Many AARs within the organization are mandated by standard operating procedures, and most employees are habituated to them.

'This is a habit and continuous practice all over the place here. Our Learning and Development team is doing a great job trying to make colleagues think out of the box and look into things from new perspectives. We always have an open dialogue and discuss all concerns, learning lessons, bad experience as well as good experience. We find this easy and efficient.' – Aziz, room service department, LAMAR Hotels & Resorts

Both companies complement and strengthen the use of AARs with the follow-up element, whereby the outcome from AARs and other mechanisms becomes subject to audit and review on a regular basis in order to ensure the implementation of the agreed actions and also the required changes in the operation manuals, SOPs and policies.

Summary

Organizations, researchers and practitioners tend to repeatedly overuse the term 'lessons learned' when in fact we don't fully learn a lesson until we implement this learning. Extracting some knowledge about an incident doesn't help much if this knowledge isn't put into action. Based on the research findings[114] and our observation, AARs overlap with the mechanism of problem-solving teams (PSTs) (see Chapter 6). The key difference is that an AAR is an offline practice, i.e. it occurs after the event or a series of events in a project, whereas PSTs may operate either during or after the event. AARs also engage reflection and brainstorming (see Chapter 2). Unlike post-mortems, however, the AAR is a continuing practice that is focused forward, generating lessons to be applied in the future by the same people who developed them. It is only through a connected series of forward-looking AAR meetings that a team can self-correct and build confidence in its ability to bring in continuous improvement and tangible positive results[115].

6

Problem-solving Teams (PSTs)

'Most of the problems in life are because of two
reasons: We act without thinking, or we keep
thinking without acting.'
– author unknown

Introduction

This chapter develops a further understanding of problem-
solving and how it can act as a vehicle for organizational
learning (OL). It explains the team context in solving
problems, and it also sheds light on incidents at work, how
they can be handled through the incident learning system
(ILS), and how the ILS integrates with other subsystems,
such as quality, listening and learning. Problem-solving
can be defined as the ability to work through problems
by using critical and analytical thinking skills to figure
out a solution. In the workplace, teams have to solve
problems almost daily. Individuals seldom solve complex
problems in the workplace, which is why teams are usually
responsible for finding appropriate solutions and reaching

specified goals. When people work together, they can share and compare ideas and choose the one that best solves the problem[116]. Based on the overall goals, various sub-goals will be identified at the beginning of the teamwork process in the course of mission analysis, strategy formulation and planning, and all aspects of the transition phase[117].

Problem-solving teams and the incident learning system

Jones and McBride[118] argue that one way OL can occur is through problem-solving. They define a 'problem' as an undesirable gap between an expected and observed state, let's call it a 'mismatch', which causes a surprise to the employees and results in an organizational inquiry to investigate both why this gap occurred and how it can be overcome[119]. In this sense, problem-solving techniques and reflection can be used to reach the desired outcome – i.e. a solution. Research on problem-solving focuses on preferable methods rather than on what happens when employees encounter a problem in their day-to-day activities in the organizational context; 'empirical research is thus needed to understand how organizations' members handle problems that arise in day-to-day execution'[120].

One may ask, does the Learning-Driven Business (LDB) need learning simply to fix issues and solve problems? We believe that learning is not only needed to build up a sufficient understanding for performing and managing problem-solving process, but also for acquiring the capacity to derive efficient problem-solving process from an organization's strategy[121]. Learning from incidents can be an indispensable source for enhanced performance at the LDB. However, in order to learn from incidents, LDB should establish a problem or 'incident learning system'[122] similar to problem-solving teams as a subset of the central listening system (CLS). We talk more about the central listening system in Chapter 11, but it is essentially a subsystem of organization-wide learning – see Figure 6.1.

To complement the picture, we propose the integration of the two systems, i.e. the ILS and the CLS, which together

FIGURE 6.1 Proposed Incident and Learning System

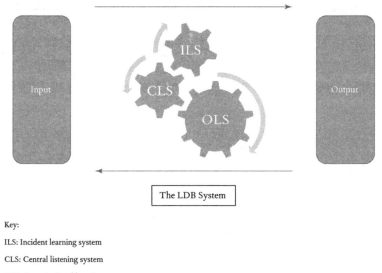

Key:

ILS: Incident learning system

CLS: Central listening system

OLS: Organizational learning system

Source: Authors.

form a vital component of the overall LDB. The primary purpose of the ILS is to identify and analyse incidents in order to correct deficiencies, which seems to be single-loop learning. This is illustrated in Figure 6.2.

Argyris[123] realized that solving problems is important and identifies certain conditions for learning to continue. He suggested that managers and employees should look inwards and reflect on their behaviour and then change how they act afterwards. It seems that there is a nexus between productive OL, problem-solving and action learning. Action learning is a powerful approach to the development of people in organizations, which takes the task as the vehicle for learning. It is based on the premises that there is no learning without action and no deliberate action without learning, as stated by Reg Revans[124]. Mumford[125] subsequently introduced a set of individual behaviours for active learning groups, such as:

FIGURE 6.2 Components of an Incident Learning System (ILS)

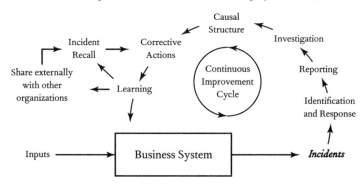

Source: Cooke and Rohleder (2006, p. 218)

1 enabling fellows to share their time appropriately;
2 avoiding being defensive about one's own actions and learning;
3 being supportive about issues/concerns of others;
4 being open to recognize and respond to issues, analytical, questioning in style;
5 listening effectively;
6 accepting help;
7 being creative in response to problems;
8 being innovative in recognizing learning from the task, risk-taking;
9 understanding and using learning styles;
10 building on the strengths of others as learners;
11 helping to motivate others as learners.

We believe that the above list of behaviours helps in understanding the nature and dynamics of problem-solving teams as an LDB mechanism. The way employees deal with a problem and resolve it can reinforce or inhibit learning. In that sense, if employees focus on overcoming the immediate obstacles and ignore opportunities for learning and change, things will never truly improve. This is often the case in hospitals, when healthcare staff resolve the urgent problem but don't inquire into the root cause of the issue. As such, the problem-solving behaviour of front-line employees may reduce an organization's ability to detect underlying causes of recurring problems[126].

Approaches to problem-solving

Problem-solving mechanisms should be adopted in a systematic way. David Garvin[127] listed five approaches adopted by businesses that seek to improve their learning:

1 experimentation with new approaches;
2 learning from problems;
3 learning from the business's experience and past history;
4 learning from the experience and practices of others;
5 transferring knowledge quickly and efficiently throughout the business.

Dixon[128] argued that learning is part of work and work involves learning – i.e. that they are not separate functions but are intertwined. This view seems to be evident in our case study company Mirage Aqua Park, as demonstrated later in this chapter. In this instance, there was a consensus that problems should be put on the table and discussed by concerned individuals, several sessions or brainstorming can be organized, and many sources can be visited as each problem is unique. There was also a consensus that there is no pre-set system to resolve problems. Indeed, it is extremely difficult to develop an automatic problem-solving system that can cope with a variety of problems. The main reason for this is that the knowledge needed to solve a particular problem will vary considerably depending on the nature of the problem.

Although individual learning does not necessarily lead to OL, it is not possible to have OL without individual learning. It also occurs when individuals within the business experience a problematic situation and inquire into it on behalf of the organization. The 'mismatch'[129] problems cause a surprise to the employees and call for an organizational inquiry to investigate why this gap occurred and how it can be overcome. The challenge is how organizations assimilate, integrate and institutionalize the learning outcomes into its system.

The transformation of IL to OL can occur extensively within the context of problem-solving. However, the transformation of GL to OL still seems to be missing or made up by other mechanisms, such as self-assessment, review, audit and AARs. Indeed, it is two-way learning, i.e. learning is needed to resolve problems and resolving problems can lead to learning since it is needed to acquire the capacity of deriving efficient problem-solving process from business strategy[130].

Problem-solving in action

In the two businesses we investigated, we noticed that problems are generally discussed, point by point, in briefing meetings. Everyone learns something from each other or from cases. At the first stage, attempts are made within the departments to solve the problems, but the fact is that some of them require extra effort in order to be solved. Indeed, a few of the interviewees said that for some problems there have been no solutions. This is because customers sometimes create problems that are difficult to completely resolve. Meetings play an active role in these cases. Information is generated through brainstorming discussions, and interdepartmental and cross-functional meetings provide a forum where problems can be put on the table and discussed. The outcome of the discussions is then communicated to other departments and units. In a second round of discussions, a decision is made and communicated back to everyone. There is thus comprehensive two-way communication throughout the organization and everyone has the opportunity to add to the information being used to solve the problem. Listening and understanding, investigation and root cause analysis, organizational inquiry, benchmarking, business excellence audits and feedback, and direct observation are among the key practices that exist in both organizations.

'In order to resolve [a problem in the restaurant], we visited many other restaurants, hotels and fast-food chains. We learnt many things from them and now we can pre-cook some items and based on the figures every day we can estimate how many guests will come the next day, and we get prepared.' – Roland, guest services officer, LAMAR Hotels & Resorts

The hotel's Business Excellence Department plays a significant role in resolving problems related to guests; it seems to be the custodian of this process, from collating information to contacting the customer to examine their satisfaction level. Communication of the learning outcome is subsequently shared with the concerned staff or business unit. Furthermore, there are efforts to standardize the solutions and amend policies as needed.

> 'After investigation of the problem we put in a solution, and we keep watching if it works, and if it works, we standardize the solution we brought in; subsequently, this requires a change in the Standard Operating Procedures (SOPs). Business Excellence will evaluate issues and classify the comments, then communicate them to the concerned departments. Sometimes the colleague who encountered the problem knows how to resolve it, so he resolves it, and he updates the others during the briefing meeting. This way, everyone will learn about the problem and will know what can be done.' – Zoe, team leader, business excellence department, LAMAR Hotels & Resorts

There is a general consensus among the respondents about accepting problems as challenges or areas for improvement. Most of them associated 'learning' with 'problems' and considered problems as learning opportunities that can improve performance. Each department has a chance to review the problem and propose solutions, in addition to commenting on and evaluating the solutions provided by other departments.

'We do not call it a problem; we used to call it challenge. Our way here is to discuss and get other colleagues' opinions. One of the common challenges we have is [a] delay from municipality to approve our campaigns. When things go wrong here, we try first to understand why it happened and why it is being repeated. Then we meet and put our heads together to find a way to resolve, prevent or at least reduce it. And the municipality is an example of this.' – Riham, public relations and communications team leader, LAMAR Hotels & Resorts

Some problems, however, need to be attended to immediately without there being a chance to discuss or interpret them. Safety-related issues are a good example of this, where interpretation, analysis and reflection come later, after the resolution of the problem.

'If we can take action to resolve it we do, especially if it is related to the guest safety or some emergency. Otherwise, we discuss the problem in the briefing meeting and seek ideas for solving it. Because in the meetings you have all the teams and you get many ideas – sometimes a colleague suggests some idea, but it is not clear enough then someone else will clarify and add to it, so we complement each other. [However, if anything is] related to the guest we have to take immediate action. We do not wait and discuss. But yes, management discuss everything in the meetings and they inform us.' – Steve, deputy manager, operations, LAMAR Hotels & Resorts

All managers mentioned that they encourage their subordinates to think like managers and put themselves in the position of a manager, whereby they can take actions and decisions without referring to their superiors. The decisions can be reviewed later for further learning and refinement. They also confirmed that they were keen and encouraged to implement many healthy practices, such as conducting awareness sessions, proposing actions and encourage their subordinates to do the same, securing resources and promoting a blame-free culture that is rooted at all levels.

'I encourage my team to work as a manager, so they have to be ready to resolve problems and think in new ways to resolve problems. All colleagues are empowered within their areas, so they know what has to be done and how.' – Michelle, learning and development manager, LAMAR Hotels & Resorts

The company has accumulated and documented experiences in problem-solving and learning lessons that have emerged throughout their history. Furthermore, the company's policies necessitate investing in employees' learning and development. For example, every employee is entitled to six hours per month of training and development. The integration of information is carried out in several ways, and we observed that the company, and especially the Learning and Development Department, is proactive in communicating to its employees and directly updating its policies and procedures. The following are examples of information integration strategies:

+ devised and amended procedures and manuals;
+ devised new policies and workflows;
+ communication through various channels;
+ open dialogue and the open-door policy;
+ Kaizen days (a campaign for continuous improvement derived from the Japanese approach to improvement known as Kaizen[131].

Acquired knowledge is validated by the concerned employees and disseminated company-wide. Action plans are approved and subject to audit and verification by internal and external reviewers. Execution of agreed actions is linked to a performance appraisal system and payment.

In summary, employees solve problems by talking and by sharing their experience both within their departments and with another department in the company. They observe customers and reflect on any incident that takes place during the day. Conversations are based on daily problems. Employees are aware that they are listened to when they raise something that requires attention. It is worthy of mention that the senior management team can serve as a role model for everyone as they have managed to instil learning culture and openness to discuss problems, incidents and complaints with one purpose in mind: learning and improvement.

7

Action Learning Sets (ALSs)

'There can be no learning without action and no
sober and deliberate action without learning.
The mark of a person is in the questions they pose,
not just the statements they make.'
Reg Revans[132], founder of Action Learning

Introduction

In the LDB, there is a variety of group and team processes that can help provide ideas for improvement and change and to solve problems. These include problem-solving teams, quality circles and after-action reviews. Each of these has a place in this book and can add significant value. In this chapter, however, we will highlight a well-researched form or mechanism of organizational learning within team settings: action learning sets (ALS).

Action learning (AL) can be thought of a subset of organizational learning. We consider ALS as a fundamental method for tackling more difficult and complex issues that cannot be resolved with quick or easy solutions. In the post-Covid-19 era, ALS need to be established more readily because they can both support and challenge leaders, managers and staff in difficult times. Mike Pedler[133] defined action learning as 'a method of problem-solving and learning in groups to bring about change for individuals, teams and organizations. It works to build the relationships which help any organization improve existing operations and learn and innovate for the future.'

The idea of action learning

Action learning is founded on the work of Reg Revans. In the 1930s, Reg Revans was studying for a PhD in astrophysics at Cambridge University, working alongside eight Nobel Prize winners. None of them worked in his field, but he noticed that when they were faced with difficult research problems, they would sit down together and ask one another lots of questions. No one person was considered more important than any other, and they all had contributions to make, even when they were not experts in a particular field. In this way, they teased out workable solutions to their own and other's problems. Revans was struck by how powerful this technique was. When he went to work for the Coal Board in the 1940s[134], he introduced the method there. When pit managers had problems, he encouraged them to meet in small groups on site and ask one another questions about what they saw, to find their own solutions rather than bringing in 'experts' to solve problems for them. The technique proved successful and managers wrote their own handbook on how to run a coalmine.

AL has since been used by groups to tackle a particular project or task, which may be set by others but is defined and directed by the group. There are also examples of virtual action learning (VAL), which makes use of Web technologies to hold meetings online and with messaging used to maintain contact[135]. During and beyond the Covid-19 era, VAL has become the main form of action learning, facilitated by advances in online technologies such as Zoom and Teams.

While Revans did not employ recognized learning theories, he did make some useful contributions, which we see as pragmatic and heuristic explanations for people who participate in AL. First, there is the key idea of:

$$L \geq C$$

where L = learning and C = the rate of change in the environment. Revans' key point is that managers must learn at least as fast as changes in their environment occur and failure to do so will lead to trouble.

Second, he suggested that learning could best be understood through the following equation:

$$L = P + Q$$

where P = programmed knowledge or answers already available to known problems and Q = questioning insight or considering new possibilities through questions to difficult problems.

Although Revans' primary action was to question the insight element of the equation through action learning, and he has occasionally seemed to dismiss the importance of P, the equation neatly captures the view that the acquisition of knowledge by itself is likely to be unsatisfactory and will certainly be unlikely to lead to subsequent action. This equation provides a fascinating question for any method of learning: is learning pure P or pure Q, or does it combine the two in some form? Certainly, in an age of knowledge that provides a ready supply of P, there tends to be an emphasis on what is known and available in codified form. If you need information about air flights or research on air cabin crew behaviour, it does not take too long to access available data. However, intractable and difficult problems cannot rely on such knowledge and this is where questioning insight becomes valuable. Questions from others in a set in response to the presentation of a problem allow the formulation of ideas to be tried at work. Such action can in turn be reviewed and declared as learning, even perhaps presented in a codified form as a new P. Others, such as Vince, suggest an extension of the formula to:

$$L = P + Q + O$$

where O = organizing insight[136]. This suggests that AL needs to consider the effect and implications of action on organization factors and dynamics. For example, politics and power aspects can hinder action, but AL can play a role in revealing the assumptions that underpin the constraints.

According to Revans[137], the relationship between learning and problems is the primary concern of action learning. It is a 'first principle' based on the logic of the combination of 1. the presence of a problematic issue; 2. salience for the learner, which together make the problem 'real'. Revans goes on to specify the possible responses when individuals have to deal with an issue that 'they do not know how to address':

a they sort through their experience for relevant concepts;
b they put concepts together in new ways;
c they seek out further information that may bear upon the issue.

The approach taken by Revans has for many been considered as the gold standard for how AL is practised, working with difficult problems at its core. Crucially, the problems need to be intractable, meaning there are no obvious right answers, and this allows the group or the ALS to work by providing challenge and support for those who want to make progress in solving the problem. It is important to add that over the last 30 years, there have been other variations on the process of AL, including a move away from intractable problems towards business-driven problems[138], and this provides an overlap with other processes, such as quality circles or team coaching.

Two other forms of ALS are possible for the LDB. First, an approach that gives more attention to how emotions and anxiety might be present in the work of leaders and others, and the need for critical reflection, involving the questions of basic assumptions and exploring, if necessary, the working of politics in the business[139]. This is referred to as critical action learning or CAL[140]. Another form of ALS allows the focus to shift away from problems towards what is working well in a business, referred to as positive action learning or PAL[141]. This allows ALS to use a method of appreciative inquiry[142] to build a picture of strengths and virtues from work practice. An inquiry process is developed to hold positive conversations about what is considered good practice. The value of this is that it allows those who seek and request positive conversations to appreciate what they find, and this can then be developed to be shared with others. For example, some key terms found in positive conversations could be:

+ Dynamic
+ Resilience to change
+ Talent retention
+ Charismatic leadership team
+ Alignment: all working to the same goal
+ Clear communication: team days

+ Celebrate success: recognition
+ Showing commitment: saying it and doing it
+ Credibility

PAL can be used to work on issues such as shifting cultures and helping to improve practices in relation to complex social problems[143].

Action learning sets

The UK's National Health Service (NHS)[144] adopts ALS mechanisms widely, and they define ALS thus:

'Learning Sets are one of a range of personal development tools which can be used to learn new ways of working, share experiences and help with problem-solving. As with all learning methods, they suit some people and not others, depending on individual learning styles, preferences and so on. A Learning Set consists of a group of about 5–8 people who agree to meet together regularly to discuss work-related issues or to develop skills in an area of common interest. Learning Sets give individuals time to explore issues that they need to resolve in an environment which is empowering and which helps the individual to find a solution – rather than be told what to do. All members of the group also develop skills in listening, reflecting back what they have heard, demonstrating empathy, questioning to help the presenter to understand the issue more thoroughly and providing feedback.'

Action learning sets are a structured method enabling small groups to address complicated issues by meeting regularly and working collectively[145]. This mechanism is especially geared to learning and personal development at the professional and managerial levels. ALS are particularly appropriate for professional and managerial-level learning and personal development work. They are most often used 1. on work-based projects where action learning set members are involved and are able to influence the outcomes; or 2. for issues concerning how specific action learning set members operate in the work context (e.g. creating partnerships). According to Casey[146], when learning in groups, individuals pick up as much about their colleagues and themselves as about management theories: 'People learn not just about their immediate colleagues, but they learn the organization's culture, which manifests itself and is experienced whenever a group of people work together.'

Casey argues that we come together naturally to play, to eat, to worship and to relax. Most people spend much of their lives in groups and learn from each other consciously and unconsciously. It is the same at work – where newcomers learn the unwritten rules from others in the organization – new workers learn the job from other workers, and managers learn from other managers. Casey presents a strong argument for the importance of learning in groups:

> 'Relationships are at the heart of managing. In addition, at the heart of relationships is the key proposition of self-awareness. There is no more effective forum to enhance self-awareness than the small learning group.' (Ibid, p. 20).

Sharifi and Pawar investigated the virtual teams phenomenon as it became an attractive approach with the increase in advanced networking technologies, and argued that 'concepts of teaming and team building have been around for decades and are seen as the means for enabling organizational and individual performance'. They presented four basic requirements that need to be present in team members in order to perform well as a team. They must: 1. have common purpose; 2. establish goals, individual and collective accountability; 3. agree on a common approach for how to get the work done; 4. have complementary skills. Castka et al[147] note that using teamwork for the improvement of organizational performance is proposed widely in the quality management literature; they, together with Nonaka and Takeuchi[148] and Senge[149], agree that individual learning is irrelevant to organizations unless knowledge is disseminated through the organization, and that teamwork is the 'core tool' for this dissemination.

Scholtes et al[150] identify a number of conditions or circumstances that enable teams to outperform individuals.

For example, where the task is complex, creativity is needed, the path forward is unclear, fast learning is necessary, high commitment is desirable, or the task is cross-functional. The rationale behind these points (with the exception of the last one) seems unclear; however, it could be tested during the data collection phase of this research. Like any other initiative, quality circles are doomed to fail if there is no leadership commitment[151]. Drawing upon the personal experience of the researcher, other causes of failure are the absence of a recognition scheme for members of the quality circles and lack of training and preparation.

Considering the similarities between ALS and quality circles, Hill proposed that organizations wishing to make a transition to total quality management (TQM) should address the issue of organizational learning because in order to improve, organizations need to change. According to this rationale, change has been conceptualized as a learning journey, arguing that OL and TQM are inextricably linked – OL has been described as a 'passport to continuous improvement'. Therefore, OL can be facilitated by quality circles (also called 'quality improvement teams' or 'problem-solving teams'). Some of the benefits of using quality circles are better communication, improved team spirit and greater employee awareness of the organization's problems and challenges. Hill draws on the stages of organizational learning presented by Garvin (1993) to argue that quality circles can help the organization at the cognitive stage, whereby employees are exposed to new ideas and expand their knowledge to think differently, in addition to their contribution at the behavioural stage, where employees begin to internalize new insights and alter their behaviour.

Why does the LDB use action learning sets?

Casey[152] argued that workgroups can provide a surprising depth of experience and understanding and have the overwhelming advantage that much day-to-day work in organizations takes place in groups. In the case of learning in groups, individuals digest as much about their colleagues and themselves as about management practices. People learn not just about their immediate peers, but also about the organization's culture, which manifests itself and is experienced whenever a group of people works together.

Action learning sets in action

In both companies, i.e. Mirage Aqua Park and LAMAR Hotels & Resorts, we observed that being a part of a team and working within a team is perceived as positive, creative and entertaining. Sometimes one person can be a part of two or more different teams. Everyone has a firm belief in the importance of teamwork and learning as a key success factor due to the nature of the business. Leaders see that reward systems are productive. General managers meet with every employee at least twice a year and their leadership is a significant motivation for the creation of loyalty to the company. Team learning has been perceived by employees as one of the strongest and most common learning methods in the organization. Team members are bound tightly, and it is understood that they closely communicate with each other. The sharing of ideas and problems is usually done at daily meetings.

> 'Our work is mainly through teamwork and this is actually what we do well here. I believe teamwork is helping [things] to improve. I myself [am] involved in four teams and that's normal here. You can see everyone is a member at least in two to four teams at the same time. All our work seems to be done through teams and committees. This is how we do our job. I personally cannot imagine working without teams. It is applied in several ways, and we recognize teams and not only individual colleagues. I think it works well for us.' – Faris, team leader, Mirage Aqua Park

Action learning sets are one of the key strengths within the business's learning system. It has two dimensions, through the formal hierarchy; the position 'team leader' is part of the organizational structure. Each team leader heads a team of supervisors/employees, through the informal and casual interaction. The interaction is centred on work, but in an informal and very friendly way – the interviewees mentioned, several times, that it was 'lots of fun'. There is promptness in dissemination of information since meetings and briefings occur on a daily basis, and, in some cases, more than once a day for the same group of employees.

In addition, there is always an opportunity to have the 'learned' information confirmed by the person(s) who generated it or, at least, by mentioning it in front of the team members where there is a chance to calibrate collective understanding of the content. It was evident that clear and unambiguous information is circulated, as mentioned, and everyone, at least on the departmental level, gets opportunities to examine or challenge information. Frequency of interaction is considerably high and consistent since the system requires that shift handover meetings be conducted twice a day – at the beginning and at the end of day.

Summary

Team learning through ALS is a very effective mechanism and is widely adopted in many businesses around the world. ALS requires support from the senior management and quality time commitment from everyone organization-wide. There are various forms of ALS mechanism, such as learning circles, quality circles and problem-solving teams. What makes ALS outcomes organizational is the commitment of leadership and the presence of an ecosystem for organizational learning.

8

Futures and Foresight Learning (FFL)

Introduction

During the worst periods of the Covid-19 pandemic in 2020, retailers operating in the UK's high streets inevitably suffered because they could not open during the lockdown. However, even before this period, many retailers had struggled because they had not been able to adapt and change their methods to meet the shift in both circumstances and the preferences of younger customers. One manifestation of these problems was the bankruptcy of such businesses as Mothercare, Thomas Cook, Oasis, Antler and a host of others[153]. During the height of the Covid-19 pandemic, research suggested that there had been a speeding up of the process that had already seen the fashion-buying habits of younger customers, Generation Z (aged 18 to 24), shifting towards more sustainable and ethically responsible sources, including clothing rental and recycling sites such as the Vestiaire Collective. Apparently, the era of fast fashion based on shopping in retail outlets is coming to an end and the future of fashion is up for debate[154]. The question is why hadn't the established retailers such as BHS and Debenhams been ready for such changes? Why did the leaders of these organizations not have sufficient foresight to predict what might happen, so that they could get ready?

It is not only retailers that are facing such difficulties; businesses in the UK and around the world are facing a future of significant uncertainty and to some extent unpredictability, which is likely to continue for several years. The Covid-19 pandemic has spurred new ways of living and working and this dynamic will continue to unfold. Therefore, we argue that in the LDB, the anticipation of the future must play an important role in the safeguarding and improvement of businesses. This is the purpose of futures and foresight learning (FFL). As we argued in Chapter 1 and showed in the model of strategic leading we presented as Figure 1.1, the findings from FFL, which usually forecasts 10 or more years ahead, can provide possible inputs for current strategy. FFL therefore assists the decision-making process in forming strategy, and this must happen on a continuous basis.

What is futures and foresight learning?

People have always tried to anticipate or predict what will happen in the future. There are a number of reasons for this. First, we might be keen or curious to know what could happen in the future – next year, next week, tomorrow – and how this will be different from current circumstances.

This can take the form of guesses or hunches or even reading more science fiction, as well more scientific and rigorous approaches. An allied reason is to reduce fear of the unknown or unexpected. In business, given the need to invest for the future, there is also a need to reduce fear of being unable to compete or being taken by surprise by new developments. Fear begets anxiety, which we want to avoid, so we try to work out how events might affect what we are planning. More proactively and, for the LDB, more meaningful perhaps, is that by considering and anticipating future possibilities, there can be better decision-making, including making investments to bring about changes that enhance performance and sustain the business.

FFL has always been an essential feature of human thinking and conceptions of time and future[155]. For many years, for most people, however, the future was a continuation of the present based on seasonal cycles but interrupted by discontinuities such as crop failure, war or the spread of virus. Fast-forward to the twentieth and twenty-first centuries and the interest in the concept of the future has prevailed. Indeed, a community has developed FFL into a field of inquiry and practice and there are now formal organizations that explore it, such as the World Future Society, the World Futures Studies Federation and the Association of Professional Futurists. There is also a growing repertoire of methods and approaches and communities of advocates, practitioners and scholars, and even a number of university departments, particularly in the US[156].

In 1911, *Webster's Dictionary* defined the term 'futurist' as 'someone who studies and predicts the future'. One problem with this is the idea of prediction, which is also a description of something that is said or written by a soothsayer or fortune-teller. As we will show, prediction needs qualification, which can be problematic.

Against the range of terms, there have been efforts to provide some clarity on the emerging field of futures research. For example, one definition provided by Glenn describes futures research as:

'the multidisciplinary study of interacting dynamics that potentially create fundamental systemic change in major areas of life over 10 to 25 and more years.'[157]

Another is provided by Micic:

'the interdisciplinary discovery and study of possible, plausible, probable, preferable and creatable long term futures.'[158]

These are both useful in pointing to a variety of influences on FFL and the direction of consideration of any work. Glenn talks of 10 or more years, while Micic considers the long term and a range of considerations. One term that is missing from both is the word 'prediction', so it appears that FFL does not deal with developing cause and effect outcomes or a single truth. This is partly a reflection of debates that are concerned with whether or not FFL is a scientific discipline or an art[159]. However, it is argued that since the future has not happened yet, it is not possible to claim truth or even reliable knowledge until it has occurred, by which time conditions can change. We argue that FFL in a LDB allows for possible new ideas to be created. It is important to add that prediction can play a key part in FFL, particularly if we give attention to the advance of algorithms and predictive models in business life (see Chapter 9).

FFL can prepare a business for undesirable events, providing what some futurists have called 'canaries in the mind', a form of early warning of impending difficulties[160]. This can be extended to include what might be called 'wild card' futures based on surprises or even more radical or counterfactual possibilities. Micic argues that since the future to some extent is unknown, current assumptions about the future might be wrong and may be open to unexpected events or patterns that take a business by surprise. This is evident in the many examples of businesses that are working based on false assumptions about the future. Perhaps the initial response to the Covid-19 pandemic was based on false assumptions too: the virus was not flu-like. Counterfactual FFL deliberately sets out to provide a provocation to a business by considering impossible, improbable and/or non-preferred events in the future[161]. For example, in a workshop with leaders in a financial services business in the UK, the following were set up as newspaper headlines to consider the future:

+ 'ROBO TOP – We Employ Robot as CEO';
+ 'GIRL POWER – We Close Our Doors to Males';
+ 'Work, rest and pay!: We open our first branch on Mars'.

Such headlines were very unlikely to come true, but they allowed for a process that opened new possibilities and also allowed implications to emerge to help the business become aware of what might happen under certain conditions – for good or ill.

We suggest that FFL can be understood as a dimension of approaches, as shown in Figure 8.1.

We can use this dimension to show that from a predictive position it is possible to work towards probable outcomes that employ methods such as algorithms as part of machine learning. Such approaches can also be combined with other methods to provide an outcome that is possible but needs qualification and attention. Nevertheless, the process can provide learning and be used in planning. From a creative position, there is a recognition that there are multiple

FIGURE 8.1 Approaches to FFL

Probable FFL	Possible FFL	Possibles FFL
Predictive FFL	Desirable FFL and Undesirable FFL (surprises and counterfactuals)	Creative FFL

Source: Authors

futures, each with a range of different possibilities, some of which are desirable and some of which are not, including surprises that are negative and provocative counterfactuals that challenge current thought. The value is the learning from working with differences and facing a range of outcomes – which have not happened yet.

Methods in FFL

The various approaches to FFL mostly make use of methods that have been developed over the last 40 years and that allow learners to make sense of data so that considering the future is not based on crystal balls or mythology. Where the learners are machines, as we will show in Chapter 9, data is used to train algorithms. For humans, FFL allows the use of methods that have been developed for strategic management but with the purpose of then considering the future. Therefore, common methods such as a SWOT or PESTLE[162] analysis might be used to answer questions such as: 'What is happening now and what has been happening?'; 'What are the forces for change and possible changes?'; 'What are the trends and patterns?'

One method that's used to widen and deepen the search for patterns and trends for any issue for FFL is horizon scanning[163]. This involves seeking in a systematic way signals relating to a particular issue. The signal might be 'weak' at present, meaning they are emerging or early but could be part of a trend; they could also provide evidence of problems or differences, such as behaviour of spending relating to different age groups. The scanning can be done using search engines. To broaden the search, key trigger terms can be employed, such as:

a people's behaviour;
b technology;
c geopolitical conditions;
d law and/or regulation;
e economic conditions;
f climate and environmental factors;
g other, such as impact of Covid-19.

An information search can be deepened by accessing data from a variety of sources, including academic papers at Google Scholar[164], as well as many documents provided by consultants, professional bodies and specialist agencies. In addition, the terms can be combined to consider connections; for example, search for 'behaviour+technology' in retail shopping, and so on. The following shows some of the trends found by a leader in a bank involved in FFL who began by considering how attitudes to financial transactions were changing:

+ logistics: physical and virtual;
+ time: rich or poor;
+ usability: advanced or simplistic;
+ customer experience: look and feel;

+ financial situation: scale of affluence;
+ ease of transaction;
+ connectivity: peer to peer.

Horizon scanning can involve drawing on the knowledge of experts and one method that can be employed is the Delphi method. This involves working with a group of about 12 experts to consider issues such as trends and patterns over several rounds. Data can be collected by email. For example:

Round 1: Gather ideas from the experts.
Round 2: Sort the ideas into key themes and confer with a pool of experts to identify importance levels.
Round 3: Rank the ideas against criteria of importance and urgency.

Further rounds can be devised to move towards a list of ideas and issues that can be considered as the FFL process moves forwards. It's worth mentioning that this was the classic way things were done in the past, before the rise of technology and new methods of communications.

Other methods of data gathering for FFL include roadmapping, driver mapping and visioning[165]. These can all feature as part of a business's strategic management. In the crossover to FFL, other methods feed the process and principal among these are *scenarios*. One of the key features of scenarios is that if they consider a time period of more than 10 years then there are likely to be possible alternatives

(See Figure 8.1) to what might happen and these can be developed as stories with a narrative structure including a plot, actors and destination. Once stories are understood as the mode, there are different ways of presenting scenarios, from scripts to theatre improvisations or models[166]. Scenarios have often featured within strategy projects; indeed, as one advocate describes them, they are part of the 'art of strategic conversation'[167] and the outcomes can be purposely employed as scenarios. The use of scenarios as a way of helping businesses was made popular in the 1970s when they were applied to help the oil company Shell prepare for the turbulence in oil markets that soon followed, enabling the business to make key decisions ahead of competitors[168].

Despite the popularity of scenarios, there are limitations if they are too central to FFL. Futurists such as Micic[169] suggest that the classic approach to scenarios can be too complex, too intensive and too expensive. They can also dominate FFL at the expense of an ongoing learning process about the future. Furthermore, they become disappointing if a focus on a scenario for planning becomes a prediction, when in fact they need to be understood as just one possibility. For FFL, the challenge to predictability has to be stated as part of the process, while still retaining the key features of working with scenarios as possible stories. For these reasons, as we will consider below, our preference is to work with mini scenarios that can be quickly constructed but still produce insights and valuable outcomes[170].

FFL in the Learning-Driven Business

In Chapter 1, we presented a model of strategic learning for leaders in the LDB as Figure 1.1. We made it clear that FFL needed to be integrated into this process. However, in most businesses this has not happened. Given the problems faced by many businesses that were not ready for challenges of the last 15 years, including the Covid-19 pandemic, it is surprising that this remains the case. Andy Hines, a professional futurist based at Houston University, was interested in why there was a lack of FFL capability in business and little evidence of its use[71]. Hines suggests that there was a resistance and a lack of priority given to FFL and too much reliance on external consultants, who might provide events such as futures workshops and scenarios but would then not follow up on the outcomes. There might be success for FFL in particular projects, but not as part of ongoing work. The challenge is to make FFL part of ongoing work and to do this it is necessary to work with people *inside* a business, who know what can be accommodated and who can work collaboratively with those who can bring futures expertise. Further, by finding a starting position that is of importance to the business, those working within a business can be attracted into FFL through conversation and persuasion. This is the approach that has been adopted by various organizations in the UK, including the example of a medium-sized financial services business (FSB) that follows.

To start with, FFL was suggested to one manager in the FSB who had recently completed a leadership programme. This manager was concerned with the strategic development of the business and was aware of the limitations of thinking about the previous 10 years, during which the business, and the sector as a whole, had come close to disaster. FFL seemed an attractive new direction to explore. On the basis that once an insider becomes interested others can be attracted through conversation, five other managers attended the first meeting of what was to become the action learning set. To quickly provoke interest, the group were asked to respond to three questions about the proposed work, which began in 2015:

1 What is the time horizon for this work?
2 What is the focus for this group?
3 What is the outcome envisaged?

A time horizon of 2025 was quickly agreed but it took longer to find the focus. As newcomers to FFL, the group members found future talk more difficult, and prompts were needed to shift their reliance on past talk feeding present talk. A key point here is for newcomers to FFL to understand the role of talk in the process and the nature of time[172]. As philosophers have often argued, language itself is historically formed and this can tilt conversations in the present in the direction of the past. Further prompting to push the talk towards the future finally produced a focus of 'The Future of Financial Services' and an outcome of 'Sustain why the Financial Services community will be here in 2025: Understand how we deliver to ensure we do'.

This process provided an entry point for FFL and a step into action learning. We suggested that to start with they should consider time periods beyond the next three to four years, which means working with what is probable in terms of the continuation of events and activities, but increasingly is concerned with what is possible, plausible, preferable and undesirable or surprising. Because the business had endured a very threatening and difficult period until 2010, and had been recovering since, it was possible to give more prominence to the way FFL could work for the year 2025. Interestingly, in the Covid-19 era, with so much unpredictability, the time period set for FFL has shifted to five years.

To respond to such unpredictability, questions can be posed that do not yet have answers. A useful approach here is to use a technique referred to as 'consult the oracle'[173]. The key here is to ask a question about the future that has an unknown answer in the present. Questions set for the year 2025 included:

1 Where will the emphasis be in terms of regulation?
2 How will people's attitudes and emotions towards financial needs change across generations?

3 Will people be able to afford to save and want to save for tomorrow?

4 How will different generations, especially the 20–40 age group, interact with the FSB?

These questions led to actions in terms of seeking knowledge from company and sector reports, various experts and also academic and other papers, as we consider in the methods section above.

The data collected formed the basis for a first review of action seven weeks later. Set members were able to accumulate significant bundles of information, including freely available documents as well as more academic papers. Presentations were made to the other members of the group. By encouraging the group to make the presentations and articulate actions in their own words, they were using language that would be more acceptable to others – a process referred to as the 'stealth positioning' of FFL. A review of learning so far had revealed that the process had:

'Allowed the time and space to start the development of an internal capability that is aligned to supporting our long-term growth aspirations.'

'Established a group of key leaders within the business to influence decision-making, using well-grounded insight to make projections.'

Once the group had accumulated understanding in relation to their questions, the next stage was to develop mini scenarios. This process begins with the projection of answers to the original questions, but for the year 2025. Projections are an important way for learners to speculate on possible answers to questions. For example, in response to the question 'Where will the emphasis be in terms of regulation?', the projected answer was: 'Regulation will support collaboration in financial services'. This allowed the development of a mini scenario, features of which are shown in Figure 8.2.

FIGURE 8.2 Mini Scenario for 2025

Friday 30 June 2025

FSB LAUNCHES NEW CUSTOMER PORTFOLIO SITE

FSB together with Partners in the Financial Services Industry has today launched a new service that will give customers the opportunity to see their own personal investment portfolio.

Working with the regulators, FSB and its Partners, including banks and pension companies, have designed a safe and secure system that puts the customer in control.

Having the ability to view all their savings and investment, mortgage and pension information from any Financial Services providers in the same place will give customers choice and opportunity.

Gone are the days of inertia and apathy; the customer will have the opportunity to set goals and pathways to help them obtain the right outcome – be that saving for the holiday of a lifetime, or planning for retirement.

Once a customer has built their own portfolio of accounts, they will see up-to-date information on balances, interest rates, risk factors and a forecast of a return on those investments.

Once signed up, all their accounts are linked together and they will be able to move their money between providers.

Source: derived from https://www.fsb.org.uk

The making of mini scenarios stimulated a growing interest and appreciation of the value of FFL and completed the first phase of learning for the group. As internal advocates for FFL, the set could now work with the mini scenarios to persuade others of the value of FFL. As a result of the interest shown in the mini scenarios and the experiences of using FFL tools, a case was made that added to the discussion around the wider use of FFL in the business. This has provided the basis for FFL to become established through:

1 the continuation of FFL action learning groups to consider surprises and counterfactuals;
2 the outcomes from the action learning being considered in the FSB's strategy;
3 FFL becoming a feature of leadership development programmes.

Summary

This chapter explains the importance of FFL in the Covid-19 era and beyond for the LDB. It shows some of the key methods and how it can become embedded within a business. We advocate the role of internal champions to broker a conversational process and seek to persuade others to join FFL. We have shown how action learning can help the FFL process.

Part Three

INTRODUCTION – DIFFERENCES BETWEEN OWL AND OL

- ✦ Chapter 9: Machine Learning
- ✦ Chapter 10: Benchmarking
- ✦ Chapter 11: Feedback Loops
- ✦ Chapter 12: Organizational Self-assessment (OSA)
- ✦ Chapter 13: Quality Awards (QAW)
- ✦ Chapter 14: Suggestion Systems
- ✦ Chapter 15: Dialogue in the Learning-Driven Business
- ✦ Chapter 16: Mystery Shopping and Auditing

An organization may know more than its members because it has a well-designed structure, procedures, policies and organizational memory, all of which are built into the organization's fabric. An example of this is the Armed Forces and telecommunication companies. After-action reviews and the learning lessons that the American Army adopt lead to a powerful organizational memory[174]. It is commonly agreed that organizational learning (OL) is complex and multidimensional. Within the term 'organizational learning', the word 'learning' is a 'live metaphor' that transfers information from the relatively familiar domain of individual learning (the source domain) to a less known phenomenon in organizations (the target domain)[175]. OL is 'an intentional process directed systematically at improving organizational effectiveness'. Some leaders will be concerned with the testing of new information and learning to enhance the performance of their organizations, while others are more interested in learning how and what other organizations are doing[176].

Most human behaviour is learned observationally through modelling. From observing others, one forms an idea of how new practices are performed, and on later occasions, this coded information serves as a guide for action. Organizational learning promotes continuous improvement, and it is a strategic necessity for organizations[177]. An organization may be said to learn when it acquires information in the form of knowledge, understanding, know-how or learning practices of any kind and by any means. In this sense, it is debated that all organizations learn, for good or ill. In our LDO (Introduction and Chapter 17), we differentiated between organizational learning and organization-wide learning (OWL). The existing literature documents only three levels – individual, team and organizational – and positions the last to encompass the learning that occurs overall in the organization. We believe, however, that OL should be broader in scope and covers what happens inside and outside the organization boundaries, while OWL is what occurs and is controlled by the organization. We mapped this to the LDB we illustrate in Figure C1, depicting the three levels as three cogs.

FIGURE C1   LDB's Organization-wide Learning Context

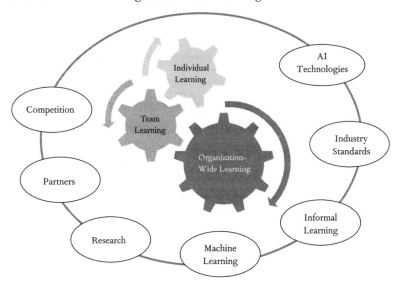

Source: Developed by the authors

In contrast, the other levels and forms of learning, e.g. AI technologies, informal learning, industry standards, research and partners, are initiated outside the boundaries of the organization but can affect the business. This demystifies the difference between OWL and OL. This part covers select OWL mechanisms from Chapters 9 through Chapter 16.

Establishing a frame of reference

Lipshitz et al[178] identify four types of learning, which they call 'learning practices' (summarized in Table 9.1). Accordingly, organizational learning mechanisms (OLMs) may be viewed from two perspectives:

+ The first is based on *who* carries out the investigation or the activities that lead to learning. According to this perspective, the investigation could be done *internally* by the organization's members or *externally* by consultants or other parties. This is related to the agents of learning or the members who collect information, reflect on problems, then draw conclusions and disseminate the learning outcome.
+ The second perspective, according to Lipshitz et al. (2007), is *proximity* to the task performed. If the investigation is very close to or happening at the

same time as the activity subject to learning, it is called *online* learning. Otherwise, if it takes place at a distinctly different time, it is called *offline* learning. In online learning, learning and working are fused together. This happens when work is attached to certain mechanisms that result in changes in the organization's routine, procedures, norms or behaviour. Schön (1993) called this a 'reflection on action' process. The four mechanisms are shown in Table 9.1.

We may use this frame of reference to classify OLMs because understanding the nature of OLMs can help in identifying the most appropriate or convenient mechanisms for learning based on the LDB size, sector and context. Besides, following the structure of OLMs can help OL professionals and LDB leaders to forge and construct new

TABLE 9.1 *The Perspectives to View OLMs*

Online/internal	Online/external
✦ Online experimentation	✦ Coaching networking
✦ Online debriefing	✦ Peer assists
✦ Communities of practice	
Offline/internal	Offline/external
✦ After-action review	✦ Lessons learned
✦ Post-project review	✦ Strategic scenario planning
✦ Communities of practice	

Source: Adapted from Lipshitz et al. (2007)

mechanisms as building blocks into the more extensive OL system. This part covers eight chapters that address organization-wide learning mechanisms: machine learning, benchmarking, feedback loops, self-assessment, quality awards, suggestion schemes, organizational dialogue, and mystery shopping and auditing. It is worth noting that the mechanisms discussed in this part are not intended to be an exhaustive list of OWL mechanisms.

9

Machine Learning

Digital machines, such as search engines like Google, can learn to do some rather strange and disturbing things. For example, it has been shown that a search engine can create and sustain ways of responding to requests that make defamatory or bigoted connections in certain advertisements against certain groups and races[179]. Just like people, it seems that machines can learn to become creators of bias[180]. In the LDB, it must be accepted that machines as well as people can learn, for good or ill.

Further, events such as the Covid-19 pandemic provided a dramatic and significant disruption to the world and a challenge to our ability to understand what is happening. As Pankaj Mishra at Bloomberg argues '...the coronavirus signals a radical transformation, of the kind that occurs once in a century, shattering previous assumptions'[181]. Crucially, what is being signalled are changes that were already in play and principal among these are the various technologies of artificial intelligence, embedder analytics, robotics and others that, together, form a package referred to as the Fourth Industrial Revolution (4IR)[182]. An important inclusion in this package is the process of machine learning (ML). If we assume that this involves the design of the technologies of 4IR to emulate learning by humans, there needs to be a consideration of such learning in the LDB. In addition, if this is the case, there needs to be an acceptance of this and action both by those involved in leading a business and those responsible for delivering learning in the business. As we will argue, learning and development professionals must become involved in 4IR technologies at all stages. This must also include attention to potential for such technologies to bring disruption to human lives[183].

Machine learning and the Fourth Industrial Revolution

The various technologies of 4IR have significant potential to stimulate the emergence of new products and services that increase the efficiency of businesses and deliver satisfaction and pleasure for customers and clients in their personal lives. This dynamic has been in play for more than 20 years. By 2019, 79 per cent of UK adults owned a smartphone, and with it its capability to support a vast array of business-related applications or apps[184]. What's more, this capability is likely to increase as technology advances towards the 5th Generation (5G) mobile network and beyond.

5G allows a connection between machines, objects and devices. 4IR technologies have had and will continue to have a significant effect on the way work is organized, performed and the use of skill, including who or what provides skill. Even before the Covid-19 era, there were debates about the extent to which 4IR will replace human skill, or complement skills or even advance them[185]. In and after the Covid-19 period, it seems likely that 4IR technologies will be more rapidly advanced. This includes its use to find ways of tackling or containing the virus but also in the way that businesses have had to respond through video conferencing and virtual events for training and so on. One possibility is the way a business becomes virtualized as well as physicalized in terms of its locational presence. Why spend several thousand pounds or dollars on a large location for a leadership development event when 150 people can easily access it via Zoom or GoToMeeting from all parts of the world? Social distancing during the peak period of Covid-19 allowed, and demanded, a reduction in human interactions and also made manifest the potential to recast work via automation, including the use of robots to disinfect rooms and drones to check on people's conformity with rules[186].

Because of the power of 4IR technologies to affect organizations, the LDB must consider how this occurs. Leaders and others, especially those involved in learning, must understand its key features. To begin, artificial intelligence or AI can be understood as any technology or system that seeks to emulate human performance. It is the exploration of how technology can be trained to complete activities that humans can do. A category of AI is machine learning, whereby a technology or a system learns 'directly from examples and experience in the form of data'[187]. ML is specifically concerned with acquiring knowledge by use of an algorithm – 'a set of mathematical instructions or rules that, especially if given to a computer, will help to calculate an answer to a problem'[188] – which works to analyse data to form patterns to then use in making a decision. ML can include the capability to automatically work through existing databases to contribute to an analysis – referred to as 'data mining' – and to work through the concepts within data to build new or higher-level concepts – referred to as 'deep learning'[189]. The working of ML leads towards patterns that can take the form of a model, which then provides a calculation to produce an output as a decision, such as the best time of day to call customers or which leads to follow up on when seeking sales. Figure 9.1 provides an overview of the ML process.

FIGURE 9.1   The Machine Learning Process

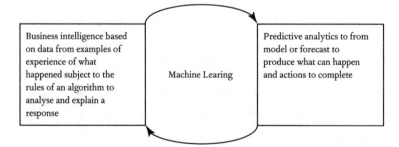

Business intelligence based on data from examples of experience of what happened subject to the rules of an algorithm to analyse and explain a response

Machine Learing

Predictive analytics to from model or forecast to produce what can happen and actions to complete

Source: Authors

ML is a process of predictive analytics. The learning process in ML is an emulation of human learning, providing an algorithm-driven machine with the necessary data to work against a goal, providing feedback to ensure it is working correctly, then allowing the machine to work out the best way to reach the goals. For example, the use of ML in sales is reckoned to be four times more successful compared to purely human processes[190]. How this learning actually occurs is not easy for most humans to recognize or understand. What's more, a machine can learn to adjust or change its path to a goal without human control: it becomes a form of 'black box'[191] to those without an understanding of data science. It also means that an acceptance of the predictions or models could be accepted without critique. For example, a model developed to forecast Covid-19 infections in Sweden predicted that 25 per cent of the population would be infected by 1 May 2020, thus justifying a strategy to allow the community to build 'herd' immunity. However, as one of the forecasters pointed out when this figure was measured as 7.3 per cent, '…the calculations are…quite wrong…'[192].

Nevertheless, ML has and will become more widespread in a variety of work processes that involve vision and speech, picture and pattern recognition, robot control, language translation and so on[193]. One common appearance online is the provision of a conversational partner or chatbot to help customers decide on a purchase. Crucially, the process is driven by ML and AI but appears as natural language, and the machine has been trained to respond in order to help produce a purchase[194]. In many businesses, key human resource management (HRM) activities, such as filling in forms or exchanging information, are part of a ML process, and it is claimed that this increases accuracy[195]. However, as we explain below, such a function is not without any risk of error. As one observer has suggested, people are 'not simply end users of big data', they also play a part in generating data, which can produce distortions such as race, sex, religion and other forms of bias[196].

The need for critique

In earlier chapters of this book, we highlighted the importance of the need for critical thinking in leaders who seek to develop a LDB. This requirement has to extend to others who have an interest in organization learning, especially the learning and development profession. A good starting point is found in the work of Noah Harari, whose book *Homo Deus: A Brief History of Tomorrow* considers the place of humans in the future. He points out that intelligence, such as the consideration of business data, is usually subject to consideration for decision-making by conscious humans, such as a leadership team. Such decisions can be made critically, with due attention paid to what is right or wrong; that is, values and morality can come into play. However, this consideration can be decoupled if the intelligence found in ML is subject to judgement by non-conscious algorithms that might 'know us better than we know ourselves'[197].

One other possibility is that ML might replace or displace humans in work situations. For example, in May 2020, journalists who maintained Microsoft's news websites were told that they would be replaced by robots[198]. Even before the Covid-19 period, it was estimated that employment in 44 per cent of occupations in the UK was falling, creating even then uncertainty about what kind of work will continue to exist in the future[199]. There is therefore a need to identify the particularly human skills concerned with interactions such as caring, creativity and communication that are needed for people to retain relevance and avoid displacement by ML and AI. With respect to the displacement of people by the technologies of 4IR, there are three possibilities:

1 replacement of human skill;
2 complement to human skill;
3 advancement of human skill.

In the LDB, we argue that it is important to utilize a combination of these possibilities to avoid the loss of human skill. Indeed, in times of social and economic uncertainty and unpredictability, in order to avoid a rush to replace human skills with ML, it becomes crucial for leaders and others to adopt a more critical and creative position. One possibility is to use the futures thinking that we considered in Chapter 8. Another is to recognize the importance of ML to bring advantages and benefits but to mitigate against adverse effects by creating collaboration between stakeholders and embedding human values within ML[200]. In the design of any approach using ML, a human-centric analytics position should be adopted that starts the process of design with the end user in mind. This requires involvement throughout ML design from those who provide and use data[201].

There are recognized ways that ML and AI can enable the creation of more work for people, such as in healthcare, where ML can empower nurses and carers in health treatment[202] by providing them with the input for decision-making and carefully assessing the possible alternatives. In manufacturing, ML and AI can create an augmented reality that complements the work of humans with instructions on parts, sensors to allow assembly, and feedback to the work process. By complementing human skills, ML and AI allow 'dangerous, dirty, difficult and dull' work to be undertaken by automation. This design of robots to help humans, referred to as 'cobots' or collaborative robots, recognizes that craftsmanship and personalization will remain important. Humans can become more skilled and productive through human and robots co-working[203]. This is also referred to as Industry 5.0 and its adoption in future years will see new roles emerging, such as chief robotics officers[204].

Such approaches in the LDB have to be facilitated so that stakeholders such as staff, unions, suppliers and others can be involved in shaping ML's development and use and to avoid allowing one interest to dominate[205]. We argue that in the LDB, inclusion of different voices matters and what is done must be good for customers and suppliers.

This also involves a critical awareness of other adverse possibilities linked with ML and 4IR technologies. For example, as we have already suggested, there are problems with how some examples of ML operate. These include Amazon's biased process of using ML and AI to rate job-seeking candidates based on CVs. The process tended to favour men because the data was based on a pattern of applications, mainly for men, over 10 years. In 2018, this process was scrapped but damage had been done to the business[206]. Usefully, this example shows possible deficiencies in how ML is formed. During its 'training', the inputs are used to 'teach' an algorithm to work towards a goal, but the training data as inputs can produce the bias – hence the need for critique of such data and wider inclusion in how training for ML occurs[207]. In addition, there is a need to critique and review how ML might produce problematic products for customers online[208]. Furthermore, the LDB needs to consider its ethical stance on ML with regard to what personal data is collected and how it is then used.

This practice has been seen as a form of surveillance that feeds profits through commodifying personal data, turning it into a 'valuable' resource[209].

Towards a hybrid professional in LDB

The introduction and use of ML and 4IR technologies needs to be considered as a strategic change management issue but also as a learning issue for a business for all its stakeholders.

At one level, ML and AI can involve discontinuous or transformational change that leads to new activities and new ways of organizing, restructuring how work occurs. Such a shift requires an organizational view of ML/AI by learning and development (LD) professionals to consider such changes as a feature of organizational learning, necessitating LD professionals to become more involved in strategic work as well as operational involvement.

At another level, in the LDB, those involved in delivering learning need to become involved in ML projects where the design is in the hands of those who develop algorithms and 'train' them with data, which then leads to applications for access by users. In businesses, the users are staff and customers. Such technologies will always be subject to different beliefs about the use of technology at work, and this requires a facilitation of human learning by LD professionals. These interventions also allow people to learn about the working of the applications of ML and the possibilities it offers for new ways of work, products and services.

At both levels, LD professionals in the LDB will need to form relationships with others who lack expertise in LD but have expertise in other domains, such as strategic work and ML work. This requires LD professionals to extend and reinvent the foundation of their expertise, first in relation to strategy but also, crucially, in relation to those who make the choices involved in developing ML and AI projects. This does not mean that they have to learn to become data scientists, but they need to be able to learn to work with the ML experts through connections and interactions with them; they develop what has been called 'interactional knowledge'[210]. As they acquire such knowledge, they are seeking neither to design ML nor to become experts in analytics but they can, over time, relate through language to others and ask new or critical questions that ML experts might not ask. This is a journey for LD professionals that will enable them to develop a hybrid role. This provides the possibility in the LDB that the LD professionals become both a people function and a people/ML function, concerned with learning in all its forms in a business. In doing so, LD professionals can establish human-centric analytics to ensure human values are safeguarded, remain relevant and, where possible, are expanded on the basis of human dignity and justice[211].

Summary

This chapter provides consideration of the inevitable advance of key features of the 4IR, in particular ML as a sub-category of AI. This advance is continuing and has been stimulated by the Covid-19 pandemic. While ML clearly seeks to emulate human learning, there is significant potential that the machine will learn to make adjustments and find solutions with little or no human involvement. There are many, many positive features of ML and AI in a business, but we have also highlighted some of the dangers. In particular, in the LDB, we advocate that leaders and LD professionals must take an interest in both human learning and ML. For the latter, there is the potential to become hybrid professionals as they learn to interact with experts beyond their traditional knowledge base. Indeed, it is vital that they do so.

10

Benchmarking

Introduction

Today, benchmarking is a key element of quality management. It is often termed as a 'hard' quality practice because it collects objective data and provides insights based on systematic analysis. It is also the catalyst for other organizational processes, such as process re-engineering and collective learning. Exact definitions of benchmarking vary depending on business context; there are more than 50 definitions available in scholarly literature itself! All definitions, however, encapsulate the same theme: the search for industry best practices that will lead to exceptional performance when implemented within the organization. A more detailed definition of benchmarking is given below:

'Benchmarking is the continuous process of identifying, understanding and adapting practice and processes that will lead to better performance.'[212]

It is rooted in the quality management movement and is presented as one of the key tools to help organizations become more 'learning oriented', adopt a more systematic and rigorous approach to problem-solving and become more engaged in learning from others. Benchmarking can inform strategic and policies planning, support the development of new products and programmes, and enable organizations to be more responsive to change. We can look into three types of benchmarking[213]:

1 Comparison of outputs or measures from different organizations;
2 Assessment against a level of performance, a standard or a range of practices and policies;
3 Undertaking a detailed examination of the internal processes that produce a particular output.

It is notable that the first and second types focus on the result, while the last focuses on the process itself and how it happens, which aligns with the methodology of this research regarding the 'how' and 'why' questions. Benchmarking, as a process, is like the quality cycle presented by Deming, involving a continuous process of 'plan, do, check and act'. Furthermore, Longbottom (2000), observes that the critical common elements of any benchmarking are[214]:

+ planning: involves internal scrutiny, analysis of strengths and weaknesses, flowcharting of processes, measurement of performance, and preparation for benchmarking;

+ analysis: involves identification of potential partners, information exchange, site visits and observations of process;
+ implementation: involves adaptation of processes and implementation;
+ review: involves reflection and repetition as part of the continuous improvement philosophy.

Benchmarking is concerned with setting objective standards and performance indicators, based on the practices of best performers, and learning how leading companies achieve their outstanding performance[215]. A survey of 700 manufacturing and service companies in northern England examined the relationship between benchmarking and OL characteristics, and established evidence to support the argument that benchmarking brings the greatest benefits to an organization's performance when it is combined with effective organizational learning. Moreover, they found a high degree of commonality between the results of manufacturing and service firms. The spirit of benchmarking and its possibilities is about learning from others' experience:

TABLE IO.I *Commonality Between the Benchmarking Cycle and the Deming Cycle*

Benchmarking cycle	Plan → analyse → implement → review
Deming cycle	Plan → do → check → act

'…is to encourage continuous learning and to lift organizations to higher competitive levels. Through problem-solving, the acquisition of internal and external knowledge and its effective implementation, standards of practice can be enhanced with the direct effect of achieving higher levels of customer satisfaction and, as a consequence, business performance can also be greatly improved.'[216]

There are main three categories of benchmarking[217]:

1 Metric benchmarking: this is based on comparisons of certain performance data, which are perceived to be both important and relevant. This form of benchmarking requires a group of organizations to submit performance data related to different aspects of their activities, against which individual organizations can then evaluate their performance in relation to that of leading performers or industry averages;

2 Process benchmarking[218]: this involves in-depth comparisons of specific areas of activity between two or more organizations to learn how improved performance might be achieved;

3 Diagnostic benchmarking: as described by Xerox, this has features of metric and process benchmarking, seeking to explore both practices and performance, as well as identifying areas of relatively weak

company performance and organizational practices showing room for improvement. While process benchmarking is an improvement technique, diagnostic benchmarking is, effectively, a 'health check' for the company, designed to identify practices to be changed and to give an indication of the performance improvements that could and should ensue.

In line with the three categories mentioned above, there are various types of benchmarking, as illustrated in Table 10.2.

TABLE 10.2 *Types of Benchmarking*[219]

Type	Definition
Performance benchmarking	Compares performance measures for the purpose of determining how good a company is compared to others
Process benchmarking	Methods and processes are compared in an effort to improve the processes in a company
Strategic benchmarking	Carried out when there is a change in the strategic direction of the company
Internal benchmarking	Comparisons between departments/ divisions of a company or organization
Competitive benchmarking	Performance and results compared against 'best' competition
Functional benchmarking	Compares a technology/process to make it the best in that technological area
Generic benchmarking	Compares processes against best process operators, regardless of industry

It is worth mentioning that the management of the learning process and the knowledge generated are at the heart of the benchmarking process. The challenge for businesses embarking on benchmarking revolves around their ability to develop a learning culture that goes beyond merely imitating existing best practice by developing new ideas and processes to improve efficiency and enhance quality, as well as striving to improve using the practices of competitors. They believe that organizational learning would appear to be an essential ingredient if companies are to optimize the outputs of the benchmarking process in the pursuit of superior performance.

Learning needs should be integrated not only with benchmarking but also with all practices and activities of any organization, since OL should be seen as a way of life for an organization and not restricted to a few practices. Although benchmarking seems to be an effective tool or practice of OL, critics have suggested that it is too slow and incremental, whereas organizations today are faced with a rapidly changing environment, fuelled by technological advances and the globalization of markets, so that traditional approaches to process improvement, such as benchmarking, are no longer adequate. Perhaps what is needed is a more radical approach, such as business process re-engineering[220], which eradicates processes and starts with a clean sheet, then uses brainstorming to create a whole new way of doing things based upon optimizing the use of technology.

To further understand the links between organization-wide learning and benchmarking, especially at the organizations who are winning quality awards – as they must have benchmarked according to the quality award criteria – a study of organizations that won quality awards tabulated the tasks and responsibilities of the various parties within the winner organizations. This is as follows in Table 10.3:

TABLE 10.3 *Tasks and Responsibilities in Benchmarking Exercises*[221]

Executive steering committee
1 Champion the benchmarking process
2 Set targets
3 Select teams
4 Monitor results
5 Support change and remove barriers
6 Integrate the benchmarking exercise with other change initiatives

Line management (middle management)
1 Participate in executive workshops
2 Help define value in their role as internal customers
3 Provide input to teams
4 Support implementation
5 Reorganize resources

Process evaluation teams
1 Conduct value assessment
2 Develop process improvements, measures and targets
3 Monitor process improvement
4 Conduct continuous improvement activities
5 Evaluate organization and manpower deployment

Consultants/facilitators
1 Help define objectives, scope and approach
2 Provide technical assistance and training
3 Help ensure conformance with company goals and objectives
4 Facilitate workshops and team meetings
5 Provide objective health checks
6 Monitor the process and keep it going

The synergy and close collaboration among all the four parties depicted in Table 10.3 are critical to the success of the benchmarking exercise.

Mirage Aqua Park

Benchmarking techniques at Mirage Aqua Park include internal benchmarking, e.g. comparisons among departments, as well as visiting competitor locations and attending international conferences.

'We feel benchmarking is critical to gain learning opportunities that will help our business to continue to be a market leader. Competitive benchmarking is a challenge at present as there are no "world-class" facilities to benchmark against in our region.' – Ashwin – senior officer, business excellence department, Mirage Aqua Park

'Mirage Aqua Park also benchmarks externally with organizations within the UAE and abroad. The focus, however, is on informal benchmarking, especially with other companies within the group. These meetings are also used as a forum for learning from other team members in the department.' – based on Mirage Submission Document to DQA, 2008

'Every Thursday, we meet with all marketing departments of the group companies; we have [an]

other 6 marketing departments at the Group. We discuss the challenges and what we learnt last week. Recently I started to take my colleagues to these meetings so they can learn and in case I am not available, they can take over. In these meetings, we do not use the typical minutes of meetings – we have a very simple one-page template that we use in all the Group companies.' – Sue, team leader, marketing department, Mirage Aqua Park

Mirage Aqua Park organize benchmarking visits to KFC, McDonald's, Dubai Zoo and other water parks in the UAE to examine common processes such as meal serving, queue processing and waiting time management at the entrance. They also benchmark externally with Disney and similar theme parks in other countries, and Mirage Aqua Park directors attend the annual conference of the IAPPA (International Association of Amusement Parks and Attractions). During the conference, they review latest trends, practices and technologies used in the industry. They bring back information to their colleagues, and everyone works together to identify relevant improvements to be implemented at Mirage Aqua Park.

'...directors visit the annual conference of IAPPA every year, and they come back with many good ideas for Mirage...Most of the senior managers attend the forum and the annual conference. We also learnt a lot from Disney.' – Ivey, team leader, business excellence department, Mirage Aqua Park

Directors and managers work with employees to gather information from several sources. This information is then shared across the organization through several platforms. In meetings, they further discuss and map the newly acquired information to their system. Some members take photographs of practices at competitor locations and post it on the Intranet for the staff to review and relate to the working environment of their own organization. To streamline business practices, the Business Excellence Department has developed benchmarking guidelines and included them in the organization management system.

'...In the past, it was not structured, and everyone was doing it individually, but now we are putting together some guidelines for benchmarking, and we have a plan for the rest of this and next year. It is important to see how others improve and how they resolve problems. Sometimes you visit some organizations, and you do not find anything new, so we have to be selective with our visits.' – Peter, learning and development department

'Jason has many contacts worldwide and he has spent his career in this business, so he knows the new stuff. GM and Management team also visited Ski Dubai and Atlantis, and we changed our entrance fees after this visit. I also visited many places overseas, and when I go there I make sure to take pictures, and I put them on the shared folder here so everyone can see and check if there is something interesting. The e-ticket was something we learnt from one such trip; it is a waterproof wristband that stores electronic credits, which can be used to buy whatever you need in the park. Simple things that make the guests' life easy.' – Ivey, team leader, business excellence department

Some practices are discussed and implemented as they are, while others are adapted to match the working environment. The following is an example of action taken as a result of informal benchmarking:

'...one idea I know, brought by a manager who visited another water park overseas, is the life jacket tree. Before that, guests used to throw the life jacket on the floor, and this was creating a mess. We implemented the idea of a nice artificial tree where the guests can hang the jacket on [sic].' – Kareem, lifeguard, Mirage Aqua Park

LAMAR Hotels & Resorts

Benchmarking is practised in multiple forms at LAMAR Hotels & Resorts and across all levels within the organization. Some practices are unique, such as utilizing a Partner Hospitality Academy, and students to conduct benchmarking and market research studies. Managers empower employees to stay in competitor hotels and to dine in restaurants in order to capture ideas for improvement.

Internal benchmarking

During our research, we found that the LAMAR Hotels & Resorts staff, especially those in food and beverages, used visits to sister strategic business units (SBUs) as learning opportunities. We found many examples of this, including the application of concepts such as upselling, empowerment and internal competition among restaurants. All staff members told us about the extent of co-operation and willingness to share information among SBUs. This was certainly an encouraging factor for internal benchmarking.

'I have been to many other places, and I always ask questions. I do it here in the Group with other SBUs like "Madinat" as they are excellent. I learnt a lot from them, and they openly share information. I learnt from them the focus on upselling training rather than cross-selling. Here at LAMAR Hotels & Resorts we give training to our staff on cross-selling, i.e. we inform the guests about other facilities we have in the hotel, and we try to sell other services to them. Upselling, however, is about upgrading and selling something of higher value or level of service. So, if they are booking a standard room we try to promote a deluxe room or business suite.' – Sonja, director, food and beverages

'Yes, I visited another SBU and knew that they implemented an internal competition among the restaurants related to the service standard. I know that it worked very well with them and I am planning to implement it here. I also visit other companies in Dubai. I attended a workshop on benchmarking that was organized by them. The empowerment concept that we apply here is one of the things we learnt after such visits. Now L&D is organizing awareness sessions to educate people about empowerment.' – Robert, restaurant manager

Academic projects as a benchmarking mechanism
LAMAR Hotels & Resorts welcomes students from the hospitality academies to pursue research projects. When applicable, they conduct benchmarking studies to help the hotel to learn from other organizations. We witnessed a study where a team of two students conducted a comparison among the top five hotels in Dubai based on predefined criteria. The findings were shared with

all the five hotels, including LAMAR Hotels & Resorts. According to staff, the advantage of this approach is that it requires no input of resources by the organization, other than time spent with the students undertaking the project.

Cross-exposure scheme

Cross-exposure is used widely at LAMAR Hotels & Resorts and is meant for those employees who need assistance to perform certain tasks or to learn new ones. It was originally implemented for new recruits so that they could familiarize themselves with other business units inside the organization and with other companies within the group. If an employee is interested in learning a new skill or in observing a task being practised in another SBU, he or she can request to be sent to the new SBU as part of the cross-exposure programme. Such a visit would last a few hours or even a few days depending on the complexity of the task. Employees who conducted these benchmarking visits assessed the results to see whether such a visit had been beneficial.

Information is integrated and disseminated through various channels and forums, such as magazines, newsletters, noticeboards, the Intranet, emails and the cross-exposure scheme, which is encouraged, supported by the management and appreciated by all employees

FIGURE 10.1   Forms of Benchmarking at LAMAR Hotels & Resorts

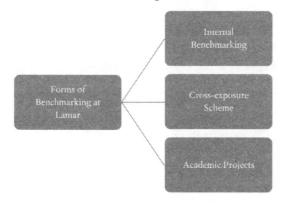

Source: Authors

because of its simplicity and direct link between the theory and practice, and the fact that it doesn't cost the organization extra money.

Although benchmarking is being done as part of the organization's routine, it has mandated, in some cases, actions such as comparisons with the guest satisfaction index (GSI) and JD Power indicators that there is a continuous effort to look into guest satisfaction from various perspectives and compare the results, to tally and ensure that targets are fulfilled. The senior managers and directors (including the general manager) are involved, personally, in benchmarking activities, which legitimize the process, add much power to its outcome and create the path for the implementation of learning lessons and continuous improvement initiatives. As stated by one of the respondents: 'it gives wings to benchmarking so it can fly.'

Enabler for learning and efficiency

In both firms, benchmarking has resulted in improvements that are aligned to other practices, such as the colleagues opinion survey, customer satisfaction index and mystery shopper exercises. Its simplicity and practicality make it an attractive OL practice for employees at both organizations. In a small number of cases, though, benchmarking has resulted in less-than-satisfactory outcomes. When employees carrying out this exercise compare what is done in their organization with the benchmarked organization, they occasionally realize that the gap may not always result in learning outcomes. However, the majority of interviewees perceived benchmarking as a simple and cost-effective way to identify improvement areas and to help the organizations save time by not repeating others' mistakes.

Several types of benchmarking activities were practised by the two case organizations, especially in LAMAR Hotels & Resorts, which has developed new methods of executing benchmarking, such as involving students in executing planned benchmarking projects, the cross-exposure scheme and several types of mystery shopping (illustrated in Figure 16.2).

Benchmarking encourages continuous learning and lifts organizations to higher competitive levels, but it revolves around the organization's ability to develop a learning culture that goes beyond a mere imitation of existing best practice by developing new ideas and processes to improve efficiency and enhance quality that has been made evident through data collected and observations in both organizations[222]. It becomes more effective and serves an organization's purposes best when it is complemented with mystery shopping. However, mystery shopping seems to be limited to services and processes only and cannot be extended to cover all areas, such as strategic planning or an organization's results, which can be covered by benchmarking.

Indeed, benchmarking is one of the practices that can be carried out in various ways, formally or informally, internally or externally, online or offline. For this reason, it is one of the most attractive practices, as was revealed by interviewees at both case studies.

TABLE 10. 4 *Number of Hotels Participating in International Benchmarking*

Location	No. of participating hotels
Africa	42
Asia	163
Caribbean	31
Europe	444
Middle East	51
North America	175
Oceania	20
South America	41
Total	967

Source: LQA website

In addition to learning outcomes acquired from benchmarking, LAMAR Hotels & Resorts uses the benchmarking index (Table 10.2) to compare itself to similar hotels in the region from a marketing perspective. As mentioned, LAMAR Hotels & Resorts has utilized information technology and its Intranet to share the learning outcomes from benchmarking and also to facilitate and follow up the planned actions. LAMAR Hotels & Resorts' Intranet has a very information-rich folder that contains 14 ongoing initiatives, tasks and projects related to benchmarking. Significant positive correlation between OL and information technology is thus evident[223]. As such, benchmarking practice has helped in improving the organizational performance at the two case study organizations and has facilitated the running of the businesses. For example, LAMAR Hotels & Resorts has directed a group of internship students to conduct a simple benchmarking exercise to set their marketing plan for summer promotions, which include some sort of market intelligence.

Feedback Loops

'I think it's very important to have a feedback loop,
where you're constantly thinking about what you've
done and how you could be doing it better. I think
that's the single best piece of advice – constantly
think about how you could be doing things better
and questioning yourself.'
Elon Musk, Founder & CEO, Tesla Motors and SpaceX

Introduction

Providing feedback has long been considered an essential
skill for leaders in the Learning-Driven Business. As they
strive to achieve the goals of the business, employees need
to know how they are doing. They need to know if their
performance is in line with what their leaders expect. They
need to learn what they have done well and what they need
to change. In the LDB, leaders need to encourage and
support employees to adopt a learning goal orientation,
which is more likely to engender feedback-seeking, as

opposed to a purely performance-goal orientation, which is associated with less interest in learning and more interest in gaining protection against negative feedback[224].

Why feedback is important

A part of Elon Musk's work style and ethics is giving and receiving feedback, even if the feedback is not what the recipient wants to hear. However, in trusted teams and positive work cultures, negative and constructive feedback will stretch people to learn new things and consider other, better, options. Musk also once stated: 'Don't tell me what you like, tell me what you don't like'[225]. The feedback loop is unquestionably part of every leader's growing process. For businesses, feedback loops are the part of a system in which some portion (or all) of the system's output is used as input for future operations. Feedback loops can be either negative or positive. Negative feedback loops are self-regulating and useful for maintaining an optimal state within specific boundaries[226]. Positive loops reinforce the strengths of the business.

However, for individual leaders, managers and staff, research over the years has shown that how feedback works is not always predictable. Negative feedback can have a negative impact on performance[227]. Feedback that is too negative can impact on self-esteem[228]. For leaders to win the hearts of their people in the post-Covid-19 era, they need to be open and share plans for the future, communicating important things to their staff. They need to do this frequently, fostering a transparent culture of giving and receiving feedback daily, weekly and monthly. Because feedback can provoke people to be defensive, leaders need to understand the possible responses of employees and the perceptions that they hold. Employees will make judgements about the fairness of the feedback, and research has shown that information needs to be clear for there to be the chance of acceptance[229].

Traditionally, this information has been communicated in the form of 'downward feedback' from leaders to their employees. Yet, just as employees need feedback from leaders, leaders can benefit from feedback from their employees. Employees can provide useful input on the effectiveness of procedures and processes and the leadership effectiveness of their managers. This 'upward feedback' has become increasingly common with the advent of 360-degree multi-rater assessments[230].

Feedback v. feedforward

According to the EFQM Excellence Model 2020, business is expected to establish channels for and sustain the process of receiving feedback from their people (employees), external customers, suppliers, partners, society and all stakeholders. The traditional approach of dealing with feedback is to start with educating the feedback givers to speak up while also maintaining their anonymity. Once the feedback is received at the business, it is expected to be analysed in order to identify the areas for improvement. Subsequently, the required actions are informed by the feedback and within the business's policies. This is not the end of the process, though. Feedback loops must be created in the system to extract experiences for application, and to facilitate new inputs into the system[231]. Feedback can provide a wealth of knowledge to help improvement spread throughout any organization. The quality management literature[232] [233] [234] reports an abundance of research on customer feedback, and OL literature addresses it as a powerful learning mechanism.

Feedback and learning

Feedback is considered to be one of the critical sources of learning, as stated by several researchers[235], many of whom were influenced by Kolb's[236] work on experiential learning, which describes learning processes as the following:

+ experiencing feedback from results of actions;
+ internalizing and reviewing experience;
+ concluding how the world works;
+ planning new steps and taking action.

Businesses that construct environments where feedback is readily available to those who are looking for it and motivate all their members to seek it will have a significant competitive advantage[237]. The LDB is expected to give feedback to the stakeholders on the actions and measures that have been taken and to seek their satisfaction. By doing so, the feedback loop is closed and can start over again. Businesses that comprehensively measure feedback are able to achieve outstanding results with respect to their customers, employees and society.

There is a consensus among researchers[238] about the significant role of receiving and acting on feedback supplied by customers and that quality begins and ends with the customer, so a pivotal role of feedback is to satisfy the customer by taking actions on the issues that cause dissatisfaction. We have conducted an extensive review of the literature and practices, and we observed that most of the feedback handling seems to be geared towards a quick fix rather than enabling long-term permanent transformation. Organizational learning researchers[239] argue that listening to customer feedback can bring a landscape of learning opportunities that can lead to performance improvement and ultimately to organizational change, with the assumption that the 'learning' is a productive 'organizational' learning[240]. When 'customer rebellion' began in the 1980s, as customers in the US started to complain about services and waiting times, some businesses reacted by tuning out the voice of the customers. In contrast, others 'scrambled to establish formal mechanisms for tracking customer satisfaction'[241].

Today, customer satisfaction has become the gold standard by which every business is judged. This tenet is supported by all excellence models, such as the EFQM Excellence Model and the Baldrige Excellence Framework – holistic frameworks for assessing and implementing business excellence. It is also supported by other quality management standards, such as the ISO 9001:2015 and ISO 10001:2008 series, which mandate devising a procedure and policy for attending to customer complaints.

It is essential to distinguish between proactive approaches and reactive approaches when it comes to handling customer feedback. In this sense, customer feedback could be categorized into two areas: 1. receiving customer complaints, which can be classified as a reactive mechanism; 2. proactively seeking customer feedback through measurement and also encouraging customers to suggest areas for improvements. For example, the L.L. Bean practice of inviting customers to comment on the new products before the official launch into the market encourages customer feedback and participation in the design and manufacturing process[242]. A customer feedback system should be integrated to systematically collect analysis and disseminate continuous learning and improvement as well as productivity. The primary objective of providing a customer feedback system is for businesses to learn from it and to make this learning organizational. Having said this, there are other views that feedback, if negative and toxic, may disengage employees and hinder their drive for performance improvement. In addition, it is a demanding process and not as easy as it may seem, which means that it may consume resources in the iterative receiving and giving process[243]. The way a business responds to such negative feedback has important implications for performance since negative feedback, especially about new products or services launched in new areas, is particularly damaging to subsequent business performance. In contrast, negative feedback in old areas can produce positive outcomes by encouraging the business to act to search for both local solutions to correct the problem and distant solutions to expand the business opportunities[244].

Considering the exponential changes that have taken the world by surprise – e.g. Industry 4.0, machine learning, AI technologies and Covid-19 – there is a pressing need for fast responses from businesses in all sectors and sizes. What's more, this response needs to consider the ecosystem and attempt to use futures and foresight learning. For instance, in the post-Covid-19 world, traditional paper-based feedback cards that involve the touching of objects will most likely no longer be fit for purpose, and besides, stakeholders are extremely busy with many other things and possibly won't have time to fill in a feedback form, even if it is digital. Therefore, LDBs need to become more innovative so they can capture the feedback in a more friendly and time-efficient manner. At the same time, they have to come back to the customer to clarify what they have done in response – the feedforward – to ensure their continued custom.

Using AI can help LDBs to anticipate the needs and to capture the concerns and feedback of all stakeholders in a more proactive manner. It should be noted that both the feedback and the feedforward process can be an integral element in the overall organizational learning system at all levels of learning and should not be limited to customers; it should also be extended to employees and other stakeholders. Jenkin[245] proposed a two-way feedback/feedforward mechanism as a core element of an organizational learning model that consists of five stages, the '5Is', as shown in Figure 11.1. Here, the feedforward goes in parallel with feedback to internalize and externalize learning organization wide and beyond.

FIGURE 11.1   5Is Model-based Organizational Learning

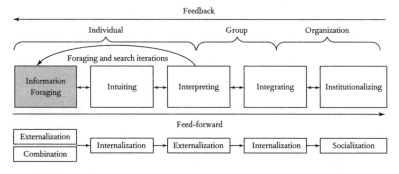

Source: Jenkin (2013, p. 105)[246]

Proposed organizational listening approach

Considering the available and future technologies, we propose a sub-ecosystem to capture and manage feedback loops both ways. The idea of a 'central feedback unit' inspires the suggested 'central listening system' presented by Wirtz and Tomlin (2000)[247], and it consists of seven feeders, as shown in Figure 11.2. It is crucial to monitor this system and to set the relevant performance indicators (PIs). However, the focus should not be only for mere measurement; it should still focus on learning activities intertwined in the processes and activities concerned with stakeholders' feedback; involvement of external support, such as consultants and research units, including industry and regulatory reports; centralization of the system

FIGURE 11. 2 Central Listening System

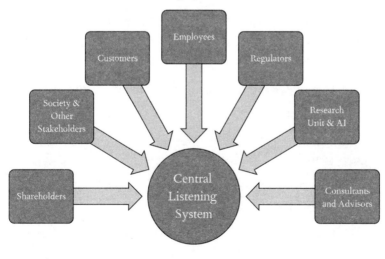

Source: Authors

189

handling; and decentralization in execution by having representatives in each business unit.

Feedback loops in action

L.L. Bean[248] has been a trusted supplier of apparel, outdoor equipment and expert advice for more than 100 years. Founded in 1912 by Leon Leonwood Bean, the company began as a one-man operation. With L.L. Bean's firm belief in keeping customers satisfied as a guiding principle, the company eventually grew into a global business with annual sales of $1.61 billion. Their company headquarters are in Freeport, Maine, just down the road from their original store. L.L. Bean has sustained outstanding customer service that's backed by a century of a promise well kept. The former CEO, Chris McCormick, attributed the success of L.L. Bean to its proactive approach towards customers and employees, saying:

'We start by letting the customer define what constitutes good customer service and then we act upon those attributes. This is really important – you can't tell customers "you will be satisfied" – they need to arrive at that conclusion on their own through the service experience itself. Our 100 per cent satisfaction guarantee stands as a prime example of our service philosophy since it is all about letting customers define what "satisfactory" means to them. We serve customers by listening and promptly responding to each customer's specific needs in a friendly and professional manner, by being knowledgeable about our products, and being willing to solve a full range of problems. On the selling side, superior service is also accomplished by providing a pleasant shopping and service experience across all channels and communicating with customers in their preferred channel or medium.'[249]

The hospitality sector seems to eat feedback for breakfast – it is one of the most acclaimed mechanisms throughout the sector. In our two hospitality businesses, LAMAR and Mirage, we witnessed a high awareness of the importance of feedback at every level, in every department and by every employee.

Mirage Aqua Park

Here, staff collect the customers' feedback at all times, every day, but in a delicate manner. Their efforts are directed to not letting the same problem or complaint occur again. New services have been developed as praxis from feedback. For example, at Mirage Aqua Park, a ladies' night service shift has been introduced as a direct result of a customer's feedback; ladies' night was a request made by a female guest who, due to cultural or religious needs, cannot wear a swimsuit in front of male guests. The outcome is being benchmarked to other standards, and the performance appraisal is linked to the result of the feedback.

'One of the success stories based on our customer feedback was introducing the lady [sic] nights that was targeting local ladies and all ladies who do not want to be exposed to men. It [has] witnessed a great success since we started it about four years ago. We applied many changes based on guest feedback. Now we are introducing two new rides as we received feedback saying that we do not have a large variety of rides. And yet there are many projects to come. Guest feedback is a big thing at our company; we listen and act promptly on the feedback.' – Adriana, learning and development manager, Mirage Aqua Park

The respondents at Mirage Aqua Park mentioned a variety of tools that are used to obtain feedback, the key one being the comments form. However, they know from experience that not every guest will spare the few minutes needed to fill in the form, so the company has developed a simple two-line card in which a guest can insert their name and contact details. The company can then contact such guests, later, to obtain their feedback and learn about their experience. Several mechanisms have also been established to capture guests' feedback and incorporate it into the work routine and systems. These include:

+ a standard form to record feedback details;
+ a small feedback card for guests who prefer not to write in detail;

+ scheduled follow-up calls for guests who leave their contact details;
+ direct daily interaction with guests, the general manager and senior managers;
+ seeking verbal feedback;
+ forwarding genuine and significant complaints to the training department, to be used later in training programmes;
+ setting a target time for response and resolution of complaints;
+ distribution by the business excellence team and others of complimentary entrance passes to guests in order to 'reduce the heat' and build loyalty;
+ linking performance appraisal and, accordingly, the quarterly bonus to targets related to guest feedback and satisfaction';
+ use of bespoke software to facilitate the handling of feedback, which every Mirage employee can access in order to keep themselves informed about the satisfaction level of guests.

'We are always keen to receive feedback from our customers. Not only this, but we also looked into things from the customer's point of view, not from our points of view. We receive daily guest feedback, we enter the feedback into the system, and after segregating them [sic], we send a report to each department.' – Pedro, business excellence officer, Mirage Aqua Park

A scored daily feedback report is generated based on this feedback, and if any topic receives a low score, it is automatically highlighted in red and given priority in handling. Once the feedback has been dealt with, the guest is contacted by a member of the business excellence team, who explains what action has been taken. If the guests are satisfied, an apology and some sort of compensation is given. If, however, the guest is still dissatisfied, the issue is escalated to the general manager, who reviews the case, decides if further corrective action could be taken, then calls the guest to explain further. The fact that the general manager calls the guest is considered to reflect the commitment of Mirage Aqua Park to listening to customer feedback.

It is evident that customer feedback, once mentioned, is like a 'magic' key that opens doors and secures resources and attention. Across the board, the company is keen to collect customer feedback and also to mitigate and prevent negative feedback. To this end, all staff members are empowered to take actions in line with their job role. For example, a waiter is able to refill the customer's drink or replace a meal if there is a complaint, without needing to obtain permission from his/her senior. Many decisions can be taken spontaneously in order to please the customer and 'make their day fun and unforgettable', which was something we observed occurring.

To ensure better learning and a better experience for the customer, customer feedback handling is embedded into the following subsystems:

+ quality management system (ISO 9001);
+ customer satisfaction index, which acts as an internal performance benchmark throughout the group's companies;
+ employee performance system;
+ employees' remunerations and compensations.

LAMAR Hotels & Resorts

The use of feedback for learning and improvement purposes was evident at this business in several forms. As explained in its submission documents to the National Quality Award (NQA), the primary focus of the hotel is to provide its guests with a unique and customized service and focus on feedback and interaction with guests.

> 'We implement this through JD Power. So, after the guest stays in the hotel and has not filled in the comment card, we send him an email asking for his feedback. We expect guests to fill in the form online. Then we get a monthly report from the system covering all aspects of our services and outlets. It is a very comprehensive report. If the guest filled in the form manually then Business Excellence collects all the forms daily and posts them into the system.' – LAMAR Hotels & Resorts submission document to NQA, Section 4

More than 20 channels are used to obtain the guests' and partners' feedback and improve two-way communication.

The following are just some of the channels that have been observed:

1 guest meetings;
2 mailing product and service update;
3 invitation to special events;
4 familiarization trips;
5 24-hour guest service;
6 customer satisfaction surveys;
7 guest preferences obtained after each meal;
8 short and one-to-one meeting during meals;
9 verbal feedback taken (even by the bellboy);
10 operational feedback during and after events (conferences, seminars, parties etc.).

There are a variety of channels that help the hotel to obtain spontaneous feedback directly from the guests, saving the guests time, giving them an opportunity to explain in more detail and also to receive acknowledgement of the issues, and, sometimes, a solution. We noticed, though, that some minor feedback that is obtained immediately after a one-off event is not always disseminated or documented, such as feedback about a meal. However, where there is recurring feedback, an investigation takes place, the issue get documented, and more appropriate actions are taken. It was also noticed that employees are being dealt with as internal customers; this concept is widespread among management and supervisory levels. The obtained feedback is subject to a complete loop where it is disseminated through emails, Intranet and meetings. As at Mirage Aqua Park, the direct involvement of senior management in most of the practices, including feedback handling, helps the business to smoothly implement the proposed actions based on the generated information.

> 'We receive feedback, and we have made many changes based on this feedback, we changed our Spa a lot based on the feedback. Not only feedback but also benchmarking exercises help us to make improvements even before guests give us their feedback, e.g. many of our restaurants' concepts have been changed based on our visits and benchmarking. We also conduct telephone test calls from outside; we improved the system a lot and introduced new categorization. i.e. in the past, everything was being categorized under feedback, now we segregate it to 'Positive Feedback', 'Negative Feedback' and 'Positive and Negative Feedback' to give priority to the negative feedback.' – Maria, guest service manager, LAMAR Hotels & Resorts

Insights from praxis

Learning from feedback at both companies is planned and structured, which is in line with the argument of Nancy Dixon[250] that organizational learning results from 'intentional and planned efforts to learn'. Both companies have developed many subsystems to obtain a wide range of feedback from its two key sets of stakeholders (i.e. external and internal customers), as mentioned by one of the interviewees: 'feedback is obtained informally daily and formally every three months from all colleagues as they are the internal customers'. In addition, a new system was being developed for testing whereby individual feedback would be obtained during in-person interaction with the HR Department. The method of implementing feedback loops appeared to us to be flexible and serves its purposes where it is centrally administered by the Business Excellence Department. However, all employees were entitled to handle guest feedback where it fell within the scope of their work.

The rationale for centralizing feedback at the Business Excellence Department in both companies is to maintain a record of all incidents for further analysis and investigation. Some of the key complaints that were perceived as a good source of learning – according to the assistant BE manager – had been shared with the Training Department after the problems had been resolved, so that they could be used during training programmes for existing and new employees. Furthermore, the guests' satisfaction level had been incorporated into the performance appraisal system. To incentivize this, the quarterly bonuses of managers and employees were calculated according to the satisfaction level of the guests, and there was a pre-defined minimum score to be achieved.

This approach may have its advantages and disadvantages. Nevertheless, since its implementation several years ago, all respondents appear to have been satisfied with it. Some of the interviewees felt that it was fair in as much that the company had empowered them to take decisions and to do whatever was necessary to satisfy the guests; indeed, empowerment was mentioned several times. All interviewees believe that feedback is important because guests are the best source of information regarding the service. What is observable here is the proactive approach and attitude towards obtaining feedback from guests and staff.

Summary

Performance feedback has a central role in the LDB because it addresses the question of when business changes and what type of changes they make. This turns performance feedback into engines of LDB because it drives their attention to learning opportunities from other businesses, and it creates the organizational changes that fuel learning from their own experiences[251].

The usefulness of organizational learning lies in its ability to create meaningful benefits for business, and its relevance depends on its applicability in everyday corporate settings. Based on our observations, responses and the documents reviewed, in both case study companies, it is evident that at least four OL mechanisms intersect and overlap, as shown in Figure 11.3.

FIGURE 11.3   Perceived Overlapping Between Four OLMs

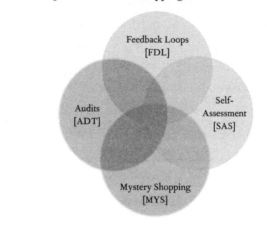

Source: Authors

The four OLMs – feedback loops, mystery shopping, self-assessment and audits – provide the LDB with an integrative approach towards learning, avoiding the superficial segregation of the mechanisms or focus on the use of tools rather than outcome and actions.

12

Organizational Self-assessment (OSA)

'Self-assessment is a comprehensive and regular
review of the organization and its results according
to the criteria of a selected model. These results aim at
identifying areas for improvement while allowing
prioritizing planned improvement activities that
can regularly be monitored. It follows that the
self-assessment model is the evaluation of the
current situation to introduce improvement
changes in the organization.'
Karol Szewczyk[252]

Introduction

A Learning-Driven Business is different from a conventional
business. In a LDB, every activity is driven by learning,
every decision is informed by knowledge and lessons
learned, and every interaction is perceived as an opportunity
for learning. In a LDB, every individual, every team

and every business unit is proactively striving to assess itself and seek feedback for learning and performance improvement. One of the proven mechanisms for learning is organizational self-assessment (OSA), which is carried out regularly and systematically to identify areas for improvement as well as areas for strengths, to improve the first and optimize and sustain the second. This chapter explains the OSA mechanism, highlights its importance and shows some good practices.

Understanding organizational self-assessment

The easiest and simplest way to self-assess an activity, process, system or organization is the tool we use at our universities at the end of the semester, where students are asked to answer three basic questions: 1. what to continue; 2. what to stop; 3. what to start[253]. We call it 'traffic review' as the green colour represents practices or 'things' to be introduced (start), the yellow represents the things that should be continued, and the red represents things to be stopped. We have used similar techniques in many training exercises we have provided, and it works smoothly. The output from such a simple exercise is often very informative and to the point.

Another simple tool that is widely employed is strengths, weaknesses, opportunities and threats, or SWOT, analysis, which can be used individually or in a group brainstorming exercise. It is another useful and yet simple tool. These two practices are a form of self-assessment – done by the employees and relevant to their business – but there are other sophisticated methods that employ holistic frameworks, such as the EFQM Excellence Model investors in people framework and certain ISO standards.

Bourgeois et al[254] use the term 'evaluation capacity', which can be described as the organization's competencies and structures required to conduct the high-quality evaluation ('capacity to do'), as well as the organization's ability to integrate evaluation findings into its decision-making processes ('capacity to use'). Therefore, evaluation capacity can become one of the key performance indicators that a LDB should consider, simply because it brings together the entire system of learning, agility and resilience. If a business is capable of conducting a structured and high-quality self-evaluation/assessment and is able to integrate the findings from this evaluation, i.e. implement the change required, this means this business is a LDB and has the tools it needs to survive, succeed and grow. Bourgeois et al. observed through a cross-case analysis that evaluation capacity tends to be higher, both in terms of capacity to do and capacity to use in organizations that have developed systematic mechanisms to institute an evaluation culture organization wide, and that having a capacity to use does not first require the capacity to do. Hence, the organization should not overly focus on the tools and techniques in isolation, separate from cultivating a culture of learning that encompasses what we call the 'spectrum of organizational learning mechanisms'.

Hıdıroğlu[255] suggested that the most crucial economic success factor for businesses is successfully integrating the business strategies they have defined with their operational actions. Hence, self-assessment is instrumental in establishing a second-tier monitoring mechanism to identify the strengths and areas for improvement concerning such required integration and implementation of strategic objectives. Kalfa and Yetim[256] stated that active management is affected by adequately measured performance and results of the performance. One of the critical success factors for organizational development and growth is establishing a system of performance measurement and implementation. We observed that OSA is increasingly applied in project-based management, as compared with process-based management; this is confirmed by Hussein et al[257], who argue that self-assessment is an important component for both the organization and for project managers to assess the level of competence using a set of evaluation criteria and an assessment scale. For the project managers, self-assessment allows them to become aware of their shortcomings and motivates them for further learning.

In 1999, Oakland[258] described OSA as a widespread technique utilized by progressive organizations. It is frequently based upon the EFQM Excellence Model, setting out a blueprint for excellent businesses by describing the practices that should be in place and the performance that should follow. This entails a comparison of an organization's practices and performance via quantitative assessments and qualitative judgements based on the benchmark standards of the model[259]. Despite the apparent similarities with diagnostic benchmarking, the assessment focuses on 'absolute' standards defined by the model, rather than on inter-organizational comparisons. The EFQM Excellence Model, however, emphasizes benchmarking as a critical element of business excellence, whereas OSA is considered a useful tool for learning and the improvement of organizational performance[260].

Why organizational self-assessment is needed

According to Lee and Quazi[261], those businesses that used excellence models as self-assessment tools had higher performance improvements, such as high levels of annual sales, market share and profits. Self-assessment improves not only operational but also managerial and strategic processes. According to Ford and Evans[262], the ultimate aim of self-assessment is to identify areas for improvement and to initiate action to incorporate changes. It has an impact on organizational learning and double-loop learning, in particular. Auluck[263] argues that self-assessment can be used at various points in the business development. For example, it can be used at the beginning of an improvement programme to identify areas for improvement and to establish priorities; it can also be used periodically, yearly or every two years, to provide comparative data and to steer the improvement programme. It can take place at the organizational or unit/

team level. Note that most practitioners recommend that the emphasis should be on understanding the organization's strengths and areas for improvement, instead of focusing on scoring and metrics only.

However, since self-assessment involves assessment of strengths and areas for improvement, Auluck conceded that a scoring mechanism can provide some quantitative measurement (even if only in an indicative sense) and that the very process of gaining consensus can promote useful discussion of the challenges facing the organization. He warned, though, that some organizations might become obsessed with the scoring and lose sight of the areas for improvement. The risk is that the business expends large amounts of energy on the self-assessment process and then has no impetus to implement any of the improvement plans. Van der Wiele et al[264] argue that organizations that used excellence models as self-assessment tools had higher performance improvements than those that used mere scoring systems, such as high levels of annual sales, market share and profits.

Nygaard et al[265] link the need to do OSA to the emerging Internet of things (IoT) technologies because the process of improving business excellence, building on IoT integration, should be supported by a proven and simple framework. This framework should consider the context and dynamics of each organization to provide context-specific recommendations for performance improvement. They emphasized the use of a framework to guide the participants in defining what is required to move from the current zone of development to the next one. The use of a self-assessment framework for supporting continuous improvement facilitates a constructive dialogue among the involved stakeholders. It is a prerequisite to establish a common understanding of the current state of organizational capabilities (especially the digital capabilities) and of common ground from which actions and development plans can begin. Without adequate and effective communication, blame-free culture, mutual understanding and mutual trust, self-assessment can be superficial and shallow, without any added value, and will lose its purpose as a learning mechanism. Szewczyk[266] argued that OSA has an advantage over certification or quality awards because its implementation does not utilize 'pressure' results in compliance with the award model.

During the Covid-19 pandemic and beyond, OSA has become necessary for all businesses. Indeed, this would suggest that there's a need to embrace the idea and practice of becoming a LDB. OSA during the Covid-19 era has been a constantly evolving process used to cope with infection and monitor precautions to prevent its spread. Backed by legislation, OSA needs to consider guidelines for safe working and is used as part of risk assessments[267]. During the pandemic, the International Standards Office (ISO) made relevant standards freely accessible for key areas, such as the use of medical equipment, as well providing guidance on safe working practices[268].

Organizational self-assessment in action

In the two companies we investigated, there was a consensus that engaging a consultant is useful. It is still a process of self-assessment, but complementing the mechanism with an external eye adds value and helps to calibrate understanding and reduce bias. There is a high awareness of self-assessment, which is systematically implemented. The Business Excellence Department is seen as the department that is responsible for self-assessment and related activities. Table 12.1 summarizes the different types of assessment, with the scope and criteria used for both, based on samples of audit report findings and corrective actions taken during the data collection phase.

'We also run an internal survey to all colleagues. Then we act on the input and feedback from colleagues. We got help from a consultant to conduct a full cycle of self-assessment based on the award criteria, and we looked into our feedback report from the previous award cycle. We used the EFQM criteria for that. We do it from time to time, and this helps us to remain focused and continue to improve our business. We benefit a lot from the audit and the report of the award.' – Shamsa, HR officer, Mirage Aqua Park

Shamsa, an employee at Mirage, believes that self-assessment is essential for any organization and recommended the engagement of an external consultant in the process: 'It is

TABLE 12.1 *Assessment and Review Practices at Mirage Aqua Park*

Review mechanism	Content of review/ assessment	Frequency
External quality review	ISO 9001 – quality management system	Biannually
Mystery shopper assessment	Mirage standards	Quarterly
Food hygiene	Municipality hygiene standards	Biannually
Finance audit	The group accounting standards	Biannually
Lifeguarding	E&A standards[269]	Quarterly
Health and safety	Civil defence health and safety standards	Annually
Benchmarking	Enablers and results of EFQM	Annually
Internal quality review	ISO 9001 – quality management system	Biannually
SWOT analysis	Sales and marketing trends	Annually
Customer satisfaction index	Guest experience	Daily
Guest verbal feedback	Guest experience	Daily
Policy and strategy review	Key performance measures and initiatives	Monthly (measures) Quarterly (initiatives)
Financial review meeting	Profit and loss account	Monthly
Business review meeting	Business financial performance	Monthly
Colleague opinion survey	Colleague satisfaction	Annually
Colleague feedback	Colleague concern	Daily
Performance appraisal	Colleague performance	Quarterly
Assessment and review committee	Performance reports and guest satisfaction targets	Monthly
VOICES	Colleague innovation and ideas	Daily

Source: Developed by the authors based on Mirage Assessment and Reviews

important for any organization, and we've done it with the help of external consultants.'

LAMAR Hotels & Resorts was more focused on agile methods such as SWOT analysis, which staff members carry out every quarter in most of its departments. The reasons for adopting this technique is that it is simple, easily applicable and does not require any training since it depends only on the 'gut feeling' of the person conducting it. SWOT has been referred to as the critical self-assessment tool.

> 'We conduct a SWOT analysis four times a year. We like doing SWOT analysis because it is easy and does not require any training; it is just a brainstorming exercise and depends on the gut feelings of the team, which are always valid.' – Yasser, restaurant assistant manager, LAMAR Hotels & Resorts

Several SWOT analyses were mentioned by the director of HR and other respondents, and were supported with photographs. It seems that this was a consistent practice across the organization, which could reflect its desire for continuous assessment, moving people away from their comfort zone and adherence to SOPs[270]. Information is extracted from participants who are conducting self-assessment. The sources are the hotel premises and internal services; employees use SWOT analysis and informal brainstorming to assess any scenario. In other cases, the criteria of ISO 9001 standard are being used to conduct a review, which is categorized as an audit (ADT). It is a very structured process mandated by ISO 9001.

Summary

The depth of the assessment and review activities sheds light on the importance of consistency in conducting reviews, as highlighted in the EFQM Excellence Model. OSA can be performed by many methods, which could be as simple as the stop-start-continue exercise and as extensive as using EFQM or ISO criteria. Conducting OSA can help a LDB to learn what areas for improvement require attention. It is also important as a requirement or 'hygiene factor' to maintain licences and to remain conformant with legal regulations. It can improve both guest and employee loyalty and satisfaction, as well as operational, managerial and strategic processes. OSA helps LDBs to spot any deviation and to bring 'best' or 'good' industry practices to the workplace.

13

Quality Awards (QAWs)

'Excellence is the unlimited ability to improve the
quality of what you have to offer.'
Rick Pitino, basketball coach[271]

Introduction

We believe that in Learning-Driven Businesses, learning
and excellence work perfectly when they are put into
action. Action is what transforms learning into excellence
and transmits the lessons learned from excellence praxis
into the learning system. Both learning and excellence
require a structured approach and mechanisms to help
bring everyone in the business on board and provide
the platform for effective interaction and organizational
learning and excellence. In this chapter, we aim to establish
the link between organizational learning and the process
of applying for a National Quality Award. There are
tremendous opportunities for embedded learning to be
gained by going through the application process, in addition

to the embedded learning in the models/criteria adopted in those quality awards. We have chosen quality awards that employ a holistic approach towards quality and we will use the terms 'excellence' and 'quality' interchangeably in this context and from an operational perspective. However, we are aware of the technical and philosophical difference between the two terms.

Evolution and impacts of quality awards

Laszlo[272] attributed the existence of quality awards to the desire of countries to assist their local industries to improve their competitive edge: 'National Quality Awards are sponsored by government agencies to emphasize the economic fact that survival in global competition requires improvement to world-class status'. He argued that the Congress Act to establish the National Quality Awards in the US was, basically, a declaration of war on poor quality. Ghobadian and Woo[273] concluded that adopting quality principles was a key factor in attracting attention towards Japanese products, making 'Made in Japan' 'synonymous [with] high quality and reliability'. They also argued that the Deming Prize[274] in Japan has proved to be an effective instrument for spreading quality methods throughout Japanese industry. A number of factors have encouraged many Western countries to introduce national and regional quality awards, among these being the success of the Deming

Prize, in addition to the techniques that accompany these quality awards, such as benchmarking and self-assessment, which they consider to have made major contributions to Japanese 'competitive superiority'. They summarize the broad aims of quality awards as follows:

+ to increase awareness of quality and the importance of quality management as a contributor to superior competitiveness;
+ to encourage self-assessment against established criteria;
+ to encourage and promote co-operation among organizations on a wide range of non-commercial issues;
+ to disseminate and stimulate knowledge sharing on successfully deployed quality strategies and their benefits;
+ to promote understanding of quality and excellence requirements;
+ to stimulate organizations to engage in continuous improvement and to introduce a quality management improvement process.

Stevenson[275] considers the process of self-assessment for awards to be one of the most rewarding and valuable improvement exercises, helping to reinforce the need for benchmarks and encouraging everyone to plan and make improvements. Jager[276] states that quality awards were introduced as a driving force to promote total quality management (TQM) in national industry, to help managers to understand best practice and to support them in their leadership role. He suggested that quality awards could be used to convince top managers that TQM is a strategic management tool, offering significant benefits and leading to better business results, enabling organizations to make several progressions, such as:

+ appraising their own progress and performance against a framework of recognized criteria;
+ supporting them in national quality benchmarking;
+ helping companies to remain competitive in their markets;
+ introducing and disseminating techniques for continuous improvement, such as self-assessment and benchmarking;
+ focusing the efforts of companies on quality improvement as a route to business excellence.

Eriksson[277] observed positive experience in companies that developed an internal quality award in Sweden. For example, it often resulted in perceived improved customer orientation, enhanced acceptance and awareness of the corporate core values, a comprehensive view of the business, a degree of participation by everyone and systematic improvement work. He also suggested that communication is a critical success factor for quality awards. Some disadvantages

215

were also reported, such as the amount of effort required to prepare submissions documents for the awards and sometimes, large financial investment in hiring consultants, which raises the question of whether small companies are able to participate in such a costly activity. In addition, there was a concern regarding the poor performance of some past award winners, such as Motorola and Wallace. Stevenson[278] argued specific drawbacks, such as:

+ award criteria are static;
+ applicants nominate themselves and are not nominated by customers;
+ awards fail to define quality clearly, which is a major shortcoming because they are unable to help organizations to reach a common understanding;
+ awards encourage a home-grown approach to quality and this will not help companies to achieve world-class performance;
+ companies may focus on winning the award rather than opportunities for self-examination, learning and improvement;
+ pursuing the award distracts the attention of the key executives from running the business.

However, the response from the advocates of quality awards is that every business is susceptible to economic downturn, shifts in technology and changes in fashion. These authors argue that organizations that embrace total quality and score highly against the award criteria are typically more robust and capable of recovering from setbacks caused by exterior factors because they possess superior management and business processes as well as better-trained and more adaptable human resources. Wen et al[279] conducted a study to measure the economic benefits of the National Quality Award in the Chinese context. They concluded that the National Quality Award can bring remarkable economic benefits, and the phenomenon that the level of economic benefits/improvement in China is less than that in the US reflects that earlier implementation will lead to more benefits from the National Quality Award.

Quality awards as a learning mechanism

Weick and Westley[280] argued that learning is an ongoing and implicit feature of the organizing process and they stated that 'organizing unfolds' in ways that intermittently create a set of conditions where learning is possible. They called these 'learning moments', which echoes a similar term in service quality called 'moments of truth'. These moments of learning, which vary in their frequency, value and duration, work as occasions when people can 'renegotiate which portion of their continuing collective experience they will next forget, render invisible, and silence, and which discontinuous residual they will treat as current meaningful artefacts of culture.'

Quality award application necessitates the existence of many other OL mechanisms, such as benchmarking, feedback loops, self-assessment and suggestion systems. The desire to receive the award and to be recognized for high quality standards might be a significant motive for most of the businesses that apply. However, we have come across many business that are using the quality awards as a vehicle for learning and so that they can receive a non-biased, comprehensive diagnosis of what works and what requires further improvement. This is called the 'assessors' feedback report', it provides a detailed analysis of organizational performance against set excellence criteria. A study by Robin Mann[281], detailed in Figure 13.1, shows that the EFQM Excellence Model is the most commonly used, particularly in Europe and the Middle East; 30 countries use the EFQM or models similar to it. The

FIGURE 13.1   Types of Business Excellence Models

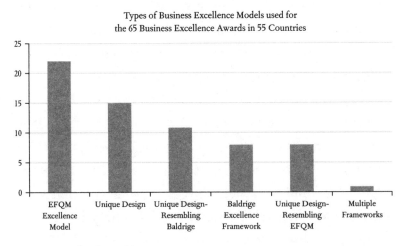

Types of Business Excellence Models used for
the 65 Business Excellence Awards in 55 Countries

Source: Courtesy of Professor Robin Mann

Baldrige Excellence Framework is also popular, with use in the US and many countries in Asia. Nineteen countries use the Baldrige Excellence Framework or models similar to it. Fifteen awards programmes use a unique model and one business excellence award in Sweden enables award applicants to choose between using the Baldrige Excellence Framework, EFQM Excellence Model or the Swedish Business Excellence Model.

First and foremost, excellence models are overarching and holistic frameworks for organizational development and excellence. The models encompass all the aspects of business, for example the EFQM Excellence Model[282] consists of the following criteria: purpose; vision and strategy; organizational culture and leadership; engaging stakeholders; creating sustainable value; driving performance transformation; stakeholder perceptions; strategic and operation performance. Second, the award process encompasses six phases (Figure 13.2), which shows how learning is embedded in the process, how learning is an outcome of the process, and that it is an iterative process. The first phase is conducting self-assessment against the predefined criteria. There then follow a set of actions. There is a realization process at work here between what is happening on the ground and what the business aims to achieve. The submission document is then prepared by a cross-function team, which is itself assessed by a team of professional assessors who are subject matter experts in various fields and cover all the criteria of the excellence

FIGURE 13.2 Six Phases of Quality Award Submission Application

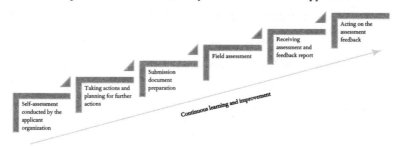

Source: Developed by the authors

model. The assessment is carried out in two stages: the first is called desktop, i.e. an assessment is undertaken based on the documents submitted at the office (desk) rather a field visit; the second is the field visit, where an assessor verifies the evidence and interview a sample of the employees. After thorough assessment, the company receives a detailed feedback report. They are subsequently expected to act on the findings made by the assessor. The report helps the LDB to realize the gap between the current and the aspired situation and take short-, medium- and long-term actions in line with their vision and organizational ambition.

Quality awards in action

In many businesses we observed, a team was formed from among the senior managers, and led by the Business Excellence Department and sometimes with help from an external consultant. The same applies at Mirage Aqua Park and LAMAR Hotels & Resorts. Analysis of the interviewees' responses at the latter indicated that the intervention of the external consultant was minimal and that the time given to self-assessment prior to writing the submission documents was less than what was needed. As such, the approach can be claimed to be formal, proactive, external and online. Building on the tenets we provided in the introduction to this part of the book, the following table classifies the QAW as a learning mechanism.

TABLE 13.1 *Four Perspectives on QAW*

Perspective	Justification
Online	The application process and related work were undertaken in real time and any perceived learning was thought to occur during the preparation. As described by one of the respondents, 'It is a realization process.'
External/internal	The QAW mechanism is classified as 'external' due to the involvement of a consultant. However, since the team involved in preparing the submission document for the award learned from each other as well as the consultant, it was also 'internal'.
Formal	A team was formed and assigned to this task as a project with deadlines and a dedicated project manager (i.e. BE manager). Each team member was assigned a certain task.
Proactive	The application to receive the NQA was a voluntary decision; case studies decided to apply mainly in order to improve and learn – and as a secondary objective, to receive recognition.

At the very beginning, everyone was informed and involved in the process by attending meetings, seminars, presentations and exams. At the submission stage of the quality award process, every business unit and most of the employees were involved to varying degrees. Employees were aware of the nature of the application to the quality award and its benefits to the organization. There was an internal (core) team with the main role of collecting the required information. Another core team was in charge of extracting the required evidence according to the award criteria requirements. Both teams were working hand in hand. We noticed that there was a clear knowledge map in place; i.e. the level of knowledge related to the awards process fell into three categories. First, there were the employees involved in preparing the evidence and writing the submission document, who knew the complete details of the process; second came senior and middle managers, who knew how to link business strategies to the quality awards criteria requirements; and thirdly, the rest of the employees, who were not directly involved in the process but were aware of the benefits and implications of entering the awards. In addition, managers perceived the process of applying for the award as a chance to identify areas that should receive further focus and attention from the senior management and to improve self-development. The act of applying for the award therefore had a stimulant effect, enabling employees to see the big picture – i.e.

what the organization is as a whole. Generally, everyone was happy and satisfied about the award and saw it as a positive motivation for the group.

Prior to collecting evidence, self-assessment was conducted to identify the strengths and areas for improvement. Information was generated from various sources, such as: previous feedback reports from the last award assessment; internal audit reports; external audit reports; consultant evaluation/gap analysis; SWOT analysis; benchmarking and performance data; industry practices and indexes; employees' and customers' feedback; complaints; previous submittal document/evidence.

'There was a team formed for this, and each member of the team was responsible for a part of the work. GM also was involved in the work. We also learnt from the feedback that was given by the award assessors. It is highly beneficial – it makes you look closer at your own process, and you see if it works or not. I believe in the value of the award as far as it is practised in reality. Many colleagues from different departments participated in the preparation; it was clear to everyone and we were informed that it requires very high standards and we did it. I think it is good for us. It helped us to realize our weaknesses. It is beneficial to us also not only to the company. We can say we have the award even after we leave Mirage.' – Waleed, officer, operations department, Mirage Aqua Park

In the preparation of the award application, the Business Excellence Department incorporated the findings from the self-assessment exercise and the information that had been generated from all different sources. Therefore, there was a high level of dissemination into the various departments of the organization, involving comprehensive communication and awareness sessions. However, the focus of the frontline and junior staff was mostly the glory and prestige of the award; it was mainly managers and team leaders who realized the opportunity the award presented for improvement and self-assessment. Although much effort had been made to raise awareness among the employees about the award criteria and the concepts of quality, and to bring everyone on board, it was evident that the Business Excellence Department was seen as the sole owner and custodian of the process. Even those who had been involved in the process of application and preparation saw their role as helping BE to execute and fulfil the task.

During the process, abundant opportunities and actions for improvement were initiated based on the award requirements. Despite this, the proud emotions created by the winning of the quality award were deemed its most beneficial aspect. People involved in the project believed that it provided support for the organization to improve in a positive direction, and they were the ones who embraced the project most fully.

In terms of feedback, the company scored relatively highly on the learning and improvement elements thanks to employees' authority and ability to take action in an independent way. One of the key methods of engaging employees across the LDB is the empowerment of staff to take actions and make decisions – something that is well utilized at Mirage Aqua Park, because of the blame-free culture that is rooted in the organization.

Summary

One of the most comprehensive and proven mechanisms for organization-wide learning is the process of making a quality award application because it encompasses several other mechanisms, such as benchmarking, self-assessment, suggestion systems and feedback loops. Most importantly, it is a useful benchmarking tool as businesses can compare their level of excellence and learning with others in the industry, both nationally and internationally. The six phases necessitate application of all of Crossan et al's organizational learning framework[283] i.e. intuiting, interpreting, integrating and institutionalizing. Phase one, self-assessment, definitely requires intuition and interpreting the existing status in comparison to the desired status; phase two, taking actions, requires interpretation and integration throughout the organizations; while, assessment and acting on assessment feedback reports may require thorough institutionalization.

14

Suggestion Systems (SS)

'One has to assume, first, that the individual human being at work knows better than anyone else what makes him or her more productive. Even in routine work, the only true expert is the person who does the job[284].'

Peter Drucker

Introduction

Few things are more powerful than a good idea at the right time; everything in our life starts with an idea in our cognition that may or may not be developed. Every product and service was once a mere idea. Every great accomplishment once was a mere idea. Exploring space or diving deeply in the deep blue oceans started with dreams and ideas. Successful businesses started with an idea. According to the company Sideways6[285], 82 per cent of employees surveyed agreed that they have ideas to make their company better. However, 20 per cent of those ideas are never heard because employees are afraid to put them forward, thanks to sophisticated hierarchies. In addition, 68 per cent of employees feel that their company lacks a structured process for managing ideas. Based on data collected from 500,000 people, Sideways6 argue that a company with 10 employees has a potential of nine suggestions a year with an ROI (return on investment) of US$47,221, while for a company with 408 employees, 335 suggestions could be received with an estimated business impact of US$94,442 a year.

Clearly, LDB can learn much from employees through listening to them – to their feedback and complaints but also to their ideas for improvement. Employees know their job better than anyone else does, and they can introduce improvements to the workplace. Suggestion systems or schemes (SS) can also play a pivotal role in reinforcing organization-wide learning and improving employees' engagement. It is even become more effective when it has automated and becomes accessible remotely via mobile phones. Further, in the UK, there are even tax and National Insurance benefits for employers who offer rewards for suggestions[286].

What is the suggestion system or scheme?

A suggestion system or scheme can be described as a formalized mechanism that encourages employees to contribute constructive ideas for improving the organization in which they work[287]. The overall aim of such schemes is to gather, analyse and implement ideas to create results that have a positive impact on the business and/or deliver new value to customers. This can be seen as a form of emergent learning to support strategy, which we considered essential in Chapter 1. The concept and practice of involving employees in improvement activities through suggestion systems or schemes are not new. An article by Carpenter dated July 1930[288] discussed the benefits of implementing a suggestion system in a school. He deemed that 'success in the enterprise can be brought about only when each member of the staff feels that he is partially responsible for the smoothness with which the school runs.' Carpenter argued that establishing and sustaining effective SS helps employees to take responsibility for their work and to participate more in setting and enhancing the organization's policies, rather than merely executing them. He emphasized that in the school, teachers interacted with pupils and with the school management. They know the issues and the areas to be improved, making them more capable than anyone else to suggest improvements. In the case of the school, implemented ideas were rewarded by a monetary award or another form of recognition. We believe this is applicable for all types of businesses.

A traditional suggestion system works centrally with a full-time or part-time scheme co-ordinator or manager who receives the suggestions, acknowledges them, evaluates them and then informs the participant of the next steps.

Employee-led innovation for organizational learning

Research at the London Business School[289] provides some great examples of companies that have made employee-led innovation part of their business system. However, it did not come easy to them: it required systematic programmes and activities to reinforce the desired behaviours, and it needed constant monitoring and championing from the top. Four enablers that can facilitate employees-led innovation are:

1 Time out – to give employees space in their working day for creative thought;
2 Expansive roles – to help employees move beyond the confines of their assigned job;
3 Competitions – to stimulate action and to get the creative juices flowing;
4 Open forums – to give employees a sense of direction and to foster collaboration.

Hence, we use 'system' because SS has to be structured in a system that is a subsystem in the LDB. In many cases, this SS, as mentioned, has an SS manager or co-ordinator who handles and oversee the entire system. In other cases, there is a more sophisticated structure that consists of a steering committee and suggestion 'champions' or ambassadors. There is no one-size-fits-all solution, but however it is done, there should be a clear structure in place for SS to be successful and sustainable and, ultimately, function as a learning mechanism. Individuals can have ideas but need others to provide development and consideration for possible use. The idea next needs a path through to leaders to provide support in the form of application if the idea is accepted. It then needs someone to make the idea happen, but with support from leaders, including any funding. Depending on the scale and significance, the process is complete if any change is managed and any obstacles are tackled[290]. In the post-Covid-19 era, such an approach to SS will need more support from leaders in a LDB to find new possibilities.

Why suggestion systems?

There are many ways in which SSs can be analysed. Cooley et al[291] investigated SSs from four perspectives: 1. the role of line managers in filtering and further developing suggestions of their reports; 2. rewards as encouragement for suggestions; 3. the choice of communication medium; 4. the role of anonymity during the suggestion process. Greeno[292] suggested that it is essential to gain insights and capture experiences from employees during roundtable meetings: 'begin with employee roundtables; listen to them share their experiences, suggestions, and key observations. This is a process of alignment and connection.' He then elaborates on the way that meetings or sessions are held by explaining that insights sought from employees must be non-judgemental. This is not the time for feeding employees the corporate mandate. It is a forum where employees are enabled to see the 'big picture' in light of specific insights they bring to the table. Indeed, the big picture can be modified by the particular ideas of the employees, and such modifications represent the learning process. The insights are fed back into the system by asking the question: 'Now that you have discovered these insights, how would you recommend acting differently?' In his treatment of suggestion systems, Greeno advocates a whole 'learning system', explaining that:

> '...when employees identify better methods of doing work, they will often suggest them to the process leaders. If met with rejection, they either resign themselves to doing things as they are told, which is frequently inefficient, or they create a separate informal process, and the tension remains.'

The alternative is to have open interaction relationships where assumptions can be challenged in an open learning environment and ideas from the bottom line can be discussed and, if deemed appropriate, implemented. Ideas UK[293] is a well-known non-profit organization that promotes such suggestion systems. The organization's stand on this is that people, both in teams and as individuals, always have been and always will be the source of creativity, innovation and improvement within an organization. According to Ideas UK, the purpose of the staff suggestion system is to promote the involvement of employees in the achievement of the organization's goals. This notion matches the fundamental concepts of quality management documented by Deming[294].

What makes an impactful suggestion system?

Suggestion schemes can become a powerful management tool that can, if properly constituted and managed, offer real opportunities for employee involvement and empowerment, which in itself is a critical component of quality management. We argue that such schemes, besides their tangible benefits, can significantly increase employees' morale. An impactful suggestion system must be promoted to all employees. This can be done through clear visual communication, such as video clips or short documents about the system. Usually, a suggestion system has a policy and handbook or a manual that contains a statement of management support that encourages employees to speak up and make suggestions for business improvement. In addition, the handbook spells out who is eligible for awards and what awards are given. The handbook or manual also defines what constitutes a suggestion[295], since some 'suggestions' are simply considered to be routine maintenance, requests, or complaints. Every organization has its own culture and needs and therefore the suggestion system should be moulded around that, and leaders should set their own policies, rules, regulations, procedures and structures accordingly.

If leaders in a LDB are able to embed the importance of suggesting and generating ideas and make it a habitual part of the organization's culture, they will sustain a vital stream of innovation, keep everyone engaged and instil pride in their staff. What gets recognized gets done; recognition is significant in maintaining positive relationships, and is a powerful and inexpensive tool for motivating employees. Recognition may have either a monetary or a non-monetary value. Most LDBs have healthy SSs that offer only small or no financial awards. What the rewards are is not always clear to employees, though. Out of 21 companies studied by Du Plessis[296], less than 10 per cent agreed that their suggestion system policy clearly explains how the recognition and rewards work. That means that 90 per cent of staff do not know or are not sure that their policies explain clearly what recognition or reward they can expect for putting forward suggestions that could have a major fiscal impact on the business. Everybody likes to be recognized and rewarded for something well done. When employees are recognized for what they do, it demonstrates and confirms their achievements. In addition, Santos et al[297] identified the following 10 critical factors that affect the success of a suggestions system:

1 top management involvement;
2 establishment of goals and objectives;
3 participation of all employees in the organization;

4 mental willingness to share and develop new ideas;

5 evaluators of proposed ideas should maintain a dynamic and proactive attitude;

6 an innovative mindset;

7 full transparency in the management of ideas;

8 outcome evidence;

9 dissemination of good results;

10 recognition.

Why suggestion systems fail

During the course of our work in this area, we have seen that suggestion systems have been neglected in many sectors and sizes of business due to various reasons, including:

1 Lengthy process – it took a long time to assess each suggestion and provide feedback to the suggesting person;

2 The application used to enter suggestions is not user-friendly; it has many bugs and is difficult to navigate through;

3 Accessibility – there are technical difficulties that make the system inaccessible or not user-friendly, such as separate user names and passwords, in addition to those of many other accounts that users needed to remember;

4 Not every employee has access to a computer;

5 Lack of awareness – we have come across companies where there was a suggestion system in place, yet a large number of employees were not aware of it;

6 Absence of recognition or insignificant recognition;

7 Lack of trust – employees think their ideas will be stolen, and someone else will take the credit;

8 Lack of response or no response – when employees log in their ideas and they receive no response, or a late response, they lose interest;

9 Mandating ideas submission – it is not a good idea to mandate 'suggesting'. Instead of pushing it, employees should be encouraged to suggest and to keep reinforcing this in meetings, via newsletters etc.

10 Some employees may think their idea is too small, hence they are discouraged from suggesting it. However, the most trivial ideas could make a significant difference. Sainsbury's is an excellent example of this: someone on the shop floor worked out that while the popularity of mangoes went up after a 'two for £2.50' deal had been offered, the packaging they came in accommodated five mangoes, so there tended to be a lot of wastage because of the odd number. Repackaging the fruit so it came in boxes of six saved the company around £60,000 – all thanks to a suggestion made to the company's 'Tell Justin' ideas scheme[298].

Employees generate ideas based on their own experience, which can be from any resource, such as: previous assignments; benchmarking activities; cross-exposure exercises; training/cross-training; research or academic projects (for CIPD, academic qualification etc.).

Suggestion systems in action

Toyota Creative Idea and Suggestion System (TCISS)[299]:

In 1951, Toyota introduced its Creative Idea and Suggestion System to empower employees to participate in improving quality by inviting them to make informed suggestions on ways to improve the production process. Previously, it had only been the privilege of upper management to make suggestions in that respect, but it was now opened up to include employees at the sharp end of production; arguably the ones most likely to highlight potential issues. Engaging employees in improving the quality of products was an extraordinary move whereby employees were looked at as more than a pair of hands and legs. As the years have passed, the system has become steadily more productive. By 1974, the number of creative idea submissions had exceeded 1 million. This had reached 10 million by 1984 and 20 million by 1988. The milestone of 40 million ideas was reached in 2011 and continues to rise.

LAMAR Hotels & Resorts and Mirage Aqua Park

Revisiting our two businesses, LAMAR Hotels & Resorts and Mirage Aqua Park, they both adopted a suggestion scheme that is known and embraced organization wide. The Business Excellence Department sets targets concerning the number of suggestions to be entered every month. This has been perceived in two different ways: some employees believe it is a good idea and it will encourage employees to bring more ideas; in contrast, others believe that the quality will be compromised in favour of quantity, and employees will start entering 'anything' to meet the target.

The principal sources of information generation are employees' experience and previous knowledge in the form of posted suggestions, good practices from benchmarking, mystery shopping and performance appraisal, self-assessment exercises, audit and reviews. Before ideas are transformed into formal suggestions, the suggesting employees discuss their ideas with their supervisors and team leaders to realize their relevance in the context of the business and their adaptability to existing practices. After the suggestions have been posted on the system, a cross-functional team reviews them and discusses their applicability in the form of an open discussion during regular meetings. If the suggestion is approved, it is moved to the implementation phase where similar discussions occur within the business unit or the team that has been assigned the implementation.

'We think of improvement daily, and also before every campaign, my team and I get together and brainstorm before setting our strategy for the campaign with a shared goal to make it better than the last one, and we take stock of every campaign to use and learn from. Besides, we have a system called VOICES where colleagues can send their ideas for improvement, and they can get recognition for that. Each manager is accountable for his or her area. I think that colleagues trust the system. VOICES is open for all colleagues, and we do receive very original ideas that make lots of improvement. I guess we implement about 36 per cent of the received ideas. This system is open for all colleagues of THE GROUP not only MIRAGE and any colleague at any of the properties can suggest ideas related to any of the properties, i.e. it is not limited to the place you work at.' – Hanan, sales manager, Mirage Aqua Park

Summary

SS can be an integrated, sustained organizational learning subsystem provided that it receives support from the leaders in a LDB. Employees are expected to be listened to, recognized for their ideas and possibly rewarded, primarily when their ideas are implemented. We witnessed many ineffective suggestion systems, and this could be due to three reasons: 1. lack of commitment at the managerial level; 2. lack of awareness about the system; 3. technical and accessibility issues. Technologies such as mobile apps make it easier for participants to have access to suggestion systems. Education and awareness play a significant role in engaging employees and managers. A suggestion system is another form of 'listening' to employees and resonates with the feedback loops in a more structured manner. We strongly believe that disengaged employees will not become Learning-Driven employees and will not go the extra mile. Hence, SS can become a vehicle not only for engaging employees but also for transforming them into learning connectors and learning agents who learn for and on behalf of the LDB and happily share their learning in various forms, including suggestions for improvement.

15

Dialogue in the Learning-Driven Business

'Dialogue is a non-confrontational communication,
where both partners are willing to learn from the
other and therefore leads much farther into
finding new grounds together.'
Scilla Elworthy[300]

Introduction

Organizations are expected to always be learning, either consciously or unconsciously. They learn with different speeds, or they use different mechanisms and activities. If they do not learn they will not survive or grow. However, this learning is often too slow and is not always associated with the appropriate response. Organizational practices and routines tend to stick, and organizational structures tend to become more centralized and bureaucratic. Among many mechanisms that Learning-Driven Business adopts, dialogue is one of the most implementable. Because human beings are social by nature, leaders can build on this attribute by encouraging employees to communicate with staff and peers to share knowledge and lessons learned. Dialogue is central to two major approaches in organizational change: organizational learning and organizational communication[301].

What is dialogue?

Merriam-Webster dictionary[302] defines 'dialogue' as: 'a) a conversation between two or more persons b) also a similar exchange between a person and something else (such as a computer) c) an exchange of ideas and opinions d) a discussion between representatives of parties to a conflict that is aimed at resolution.'

In order to occur, dialogue requires two or more parties. These parties are expected to have a means of communication and to have a purpose, which can be formal or informal. Dialogue can contribute not only to resolving conflicts but also to creating, disseminating and utilizing organizational learning at all levels – individual, team and organization-wide. Nancy Dixon[303] defines organizational dialogue as: 'an interaction in collective settings that result in mutual learning upon which the organization can act. A specific kind of organizational talk; that reveals our meaning structures to each other. When that happens, we learn and our partners in Dialogue learn as well.' In this definition, there is an obvious assumption that dialogue is meant for learning and reaching an outcome and that both or all parties will benefit and learn from this interaction. However, this does not seem to be the case in all organizations. We differentiate between general businesses where 'things' happen as usual and between those that are Learning-Driven Businesses – where learning is planned, deliberate and purposeful – and where dialogue is even more relevant. In LDB, dialogue is meant to exchange knowledge and wisdom and also to calibrate understanding and reinforced proper diagnosis of issues that occurs in the workplace. Dialogue helps employees to learn from each other and to make sense of what they face at work. The importance of dialogue has been emphasized in standards such as Investors in People and EFQM Model.

The EFQM Model[304] emphasizes the importance of dialogue not only among employees but also with partners and customers – building and maintaining relationships based on openness and transparency. The model requests that organizations strive to attain excellence by understanding the communication needs of their people and use appropriate strategies and tools to maintain a dialogue throughout the organization. A number of practices are suggested, such as: identifying communication needs; placement of strategies and plans based on these needs; development and use of top-down, bottom-up and horizontal channels; identification of opportunities when best practices and knowledge can be shared.

Dialogue clearly is associated with the term 'communication'. However, this term itself needs some attention. For example, is a leader communicating if he or she sends out an email to everyone at work or posts a video talk on the Intranet? During the Covid-19 pandemic and beyond, when insecurity and uncertainty have become common, leaders are advised to communicate often, frequently and honestly[305]. However, leaders can try as hard as they like to communicate, but this will be of little use if others do not listen, understand or respond; they might even choose to misunderstand or ignore what is being said. Leaders therefore need to be reminded that the word 'communication' in English is derived from the Latin word *communicare,* which is concerned with imparting information to share and most importantly to 'make common'. Communication is a social and communal process between people (and recently machines) to arrive at a joint meaning. In other words, it takes two to tango!

Of course, leaders have to make decisions and in difficult times, such as the Covid-19 era, they have the power to impose meaning on others. However, this makes dialogue for joint meaning difficult and also reduces the possibility for new solutions to problems to emerge from a collaborative process. In addition, leaders need to remember that employees may have their own interpretations of things and events. If leaders are not proactively seeking understanding and dialogue with employees, there will be always a gap in perceptions and understanding. Leaders need to remember Paul Watzlawick's first axiom of communication: one cannot not communicate[306].

Madzar[307] drew a picture of organizational communication where employees communicate and seek feedback from their supervisors, managers seek feedback from their reports and peers seek feedback and communicate with one another. Further, people whose aim is to learn often make great efforts to seek feedback. Such people proactively seek feedback because it can help them to gain more clarity, achieve their goals, enhance their competencies, protect their self-esteem and give others a good impression. It is likely that employees who do this usually take less time to complete tasks compared to those who do not seek feedback or engage in dialogue. One can argue that poor performers rarely seek feedback. This can be attributed to people's perceptions that doing so will be considered as a sign of weakness or a lack of self-confidence. This thought echoes what many researchers have argued about the work environment, which can encourage or inhibit learning, and the culture of fear and blame.

Maurer[308] argued that dialogue is central to disseminating organizational learning, and it can become a vehicle for the creation of a shared/collective understanding and meaning. To this end, when engaging in dialogue, participants should be willing to listen; they should be accessible in an open and transparent environment. Supported by human resource and learning and development staff, chief learning officers can play a significant role in devising dialogue-based learning through skillful and creative methods.

Why dialogue is important

It is very important to establish and maintain dialogue organization wide internally and externally, between the management and employees, and among employees and each other across the business functions. Peter Senge in 1990[309] emphasized the dialogue inside organizations as one of the five disciplines for a learning organization. He drew on the work of physicist David Bohm to highlight how some conversations are able to take us 'in directions we could never have imagined nor planned in advance.' For Senge, dialogue requires that:

1 all participants must 'suspend' their assumptions, literally to hold them 'as if suspended before us';
2 all participants must regard one another as colleagues;
3 there must be a 'facilitator' who 'holds the context' of dialogue[310].

Brockbank et al[311] argue that dialogue between people can occur naturally in organizations. They suggest, however, that dialogue should be formalized or structured for the maximum effect. Dialogue process demands structured time, space and tolerance of uncertainty.

Usually, we develop and communicate our assumptions and beliefs about life and the world around us, our experience and our work. We genuinely defend these assumptions and beliefs when they are challenged, whether with words or body language. This is because these assumptions are derived from our experiences; they are deeply embedded in our memory and consciousness. For each of us, they are 'givens' or 'truths'[312]. When we communicate with others, these assumptions operate in our minds, even though we may not be aware of them. As a result, more often than not, a group discussion consists of everyone presenting their views. It is a significant challenge to dismantle these beliefs and attitudes, especially when they have been our truths for a long time.

In Chapter 2, we considered the surfacing of assumptions through a process based on the work of Stephen Toulmin[313], based on declaring a claim as an 'I believe' statement followed by considering the evidence for the claim. Thus a claim that 'I believe it is safe to return to work' following the lockdown in the Covid-19 period could be evidenced by use of a 'Government Guidelines' document. However, this requires consideration of assumptions that are now in view, such as:

a the government guidelines are safe or accurate;
b the guidelines are trusted;
c I believe official sources rather than how staff feel.

Indeed, just these kinds of considerations had to be explored by an owner of an office-based business and two of his staff, when the staff felt unsafe about returning to work. The considerations process allowed both sides to find a more flexible approach to returning to the office.

This process can also be applied by leaders at strategic levels where statements of intent contained within the strategy can be formed as 'We believe' statements. For example, in an engineering business, a key element of the strategy was stated as:

'We put the customer at the heart of our business, providing a compelling and differentiated proposition that resonates with our customers and makes them want to become and remain our customers.'

This was used to generate a number of claims, including:

+ we believe our customers are loyal to us;
+ we believe we are customer driven.

These claims were then examined for evidence or data. They also set counter-claims, such as 'We believe our customers are ambivalent' or 'We believe we are mostly production driven'. Such counter-claims were used to create a dialogic tension with the original claims, allowing the opening of new views and reflection on the validity of the strategy. As a result, the leaders realized the importance of both production *and* consumers to its future[314].

Dialogue provides an opportunity to increase critical skills in LDB, take some risks and be more confident through a more diversified context. Through dialogue, you can not only learn about individual differences and personal experiences, but you can also begin to understand how work is structured, and people behave and why they do what they do. Dialogue provides a unique process that can hold up the mirror to the business's policies and practices through learning about employees' experiences. A dialogue group is a crucial strategy for dismantling stereotypes, improving working relationships between different people organization wide, and understanding how organizational practices affect different groups and business units.

How dialogue mechanism works in the LDB

Anne Lane[315] proposed a dialogic ladder approach to show that dialogue is not as simple as may be thought; it can take various forms and has several levels of maturity. She sketched the maturity levels into a ladder that has five steps/levels:

1. ticking the boxes – two-way communication i.e. single interaction;
2. closing the loop – two-way communication, i.e. interaction and responses;

3 shallow dialogue;

4 characteristics of true dialogue, i.e. mutuality and commitment;

5 true dialogue that includes all features of having the highest maturity of dialogue.

Another form of dialogue is introduced by Harmon et al., who proposed contextual mapping[316] as a technique that can help consultants to learn about the client, i.e. the business. However, contextual mapping is not limited only to consultants; it can be used by a LDB at any level and context. Dialogue can be practised in basic ways – i.e. limited to conversations and two-way communication or, as recommended by authors such as Dixon and Lane, structured and backed by tools and techniques that facilitate the extraction of knowledge, bring fun and leverage the dialogue. Hence, context mapping can play an instrumental role.

Context mapping is a technique that falls in the category of generative techniques, allowing us as designers to get to a deeper understanding of what users know, feel and dream. In generative techniques, users actively participate in generating ideas that can serve as a starting point for the design process[317].

Complementing dialogue with generative techniques such as context mapping is needed in order to reach deeper levels of knowledge, since employees are not necessarily aware of their everyday experiences. Interviews can help to find out what people say and think. Observations can help to find out what people do and how they do it. However, generative techniques such as context mapping can help to find out what people know, feel and aspire to[318].

Dialogue in action

The interaction within Mirage Aqua Park seems to be very strong and vivid, employing the assistance of various communication tools. The company focuses on the context and communication more than on deep organizational dialogue due to the transactional nature of business. Some of the tools they use for multilateral communication include:

1 radio: often used for instant communication during operations;
2 Intranet: accessed by all employees;
3 email: used for issues and day-to-day communication;
4 interactive TV screens: used for announcements, communication of policies and procedures;
5 newsletters: used for the announcement of company news in general;
6 meetings: conducted daily, weekly, monthly and quarterly among team members, teams or committees;
7 voice system: used to share ideas and implementation of new projects for organizational development;

8 anonymous line: employees can, anonymously, submit complaints, grievances or any other communication using this;

9 morning meetings: these are seen as the most productive method of all.

Removing any barriers or boundaries between employees is welcomed in the organization. There are several communication methods implemented in the system, and everyone has the ability to communicate any subject with anybody. Top-down, bottom-up, horizontally – there are no strict rules in the communication process. There is thus clear horizontal communication among employees, departments and business units and vertical communication between management levels. This system has been cascaded to customers, too: Mirage Aqua Park has taken many actions to embed such a practice into its relationship with customers, and this is evident on the social network websites.

'The best method for learning is the morning briefing meeting because you get to know everything that happened yesterday. During the day, you focus only on your job like I focus on the kids and make sure they are safe and enjoying their day. Things happen in other areas of the park that I do not know [about]. When they explain how they solved some problems you get to know this, and if it happens to you,

you know what to do.' – Neevah, training manager, Mirage Aqua Park

'I think team meetings and group discussions are the best because teams are formed from several departments. Besides, when a colleague in the team learns something, he can share it in his department. We have several methods and committees that facilitate learning and sharing knowledge among colleagues. It works well, and we keep improving it. I think there is a good balance of communication methods.' – Atef, lifeguard, Mirage Aqua Park

According to the NQA's Assessment Report[319], there was clear evidence that Mirage Aqua Park has several communication channels that have been made available to employees. In addition, written communication policies are laid out in the SOPs. The communication is evident from the very first interaction/contact at the park. It is not only mandated by the management system but it is also embedded in the daily routine; it has become a habit of the entire workforce.

Similar to Mirage Aqua Park, LAMAR Hotels & Resorts has adopted clear and direct communication channels that facilitate interaction. However, key forums such as briefing meetings and emails were found to be focused on departmental communication rather than being implemented organization wide. Several channels are used for dialogue: visual communication is extensively evident in all corners of the organization, briefings, twice-daily team meetings, one-to-one meetings, emails, newsletters, an in-house magazine, departmental newsletters, TV and LCD screens, kiosk computer stations, open-door policy, internal broadcasting and radio are effectively used.

'We have the monthly forums, weekly forums and focus groups. We also send monthly newsletters to all employees covering everything during the week and some hints for areas to focus on during the next week. We take much of the content of this newsletter from the daily briefing meetings and then it is used in the briefing meeting.' – Nabil, team leader, food and housekeeping, LAMAR Hotels & Resorts

Summary

The learning process involves dialogue, which in its basic form can be described as 'multilateral communication activities that make meaning'. Dialogue should be effective for improvement or transformation in a business – a theory that is confirmed by the argument of many researchers, such as Argyris and Schön[320], that productive organizational learning requires effective communication. Employees who proactively communicate and seek feedback usually take less time to complete a task compared to those who do not seek to effectively communicate. Dialogue is central to dissemination of organizational learning, and it can become a vehicle for the creation of a shared or collective understanding and meaning. This has become ever more essential in the Covid-19 era and beyond.

16

Mystery Shopping and Auditing

'Mystery Shopping is objective, unbiased feedback
from trained "customers" – mystery shoppers – to
measure how organizations deliver on Brand Promises
across markets, touchpoints and channels – physical,
phone and digital'[321]
Ipsos

Introduction

Mystery shopping is a highly effective way of measuring
and developing sales, service and customer experience
performance. In this mechanism, a trained shopper
completes a transaction as a typical customer while paying
attention to predetermined areas of focus, such as setting,
products and employees. There are various ways in which
this can be done, such as in-person, or via email, live chat,
telephone, social media or the company's website. After
the interaction, the mystery shopper evaluates his or her
experience against the predefined criteria. Although the

employees know that they are going to be assessed, they do not know how or when the evaluation will take place; hence, this approach ensures a more genuine interaction and evaluation[322].

Performance in People[323], a UK-based company, claim that mystery shopping is used not only to measure the service compliance, process and environmental performance of an outlet but also to gain insight into behavioural contributors. This is important, since behaviour is a crucial element in delivering excellent customer experience. We have discovered that mystery shopping (MYS) can be used as a mechanism for organization-wide learning. Furthermore, it can be both a useful market research tool and an instrumental LDB mechanism. It is also relatively similar to auditing, which is why we brought them together in this chapter.

Why use mystery shopping?

The Mystery Shopping Professional Association (MSPA)[324] estimates that global mystery shopping turnover is more than $2 billion, with the US accounting for half of it and Europe around 25 per cent. Despite this, it is likely that only a few mystery shopping-focused companies (both MSPA and non-MSPA members) exist. However, it is difficult to provide an accurate estimate as MYS is practised across the world. Informed by our thorough research, we can say that mystery shopping is an under-developed area in terms of research and publications, which makes it difficult to provide accurate figures about the size of MYS practice.

This practice of MYS is widely adopted in sectors such as retail, hospitality, insurance, banking, airlines, healthcare and government. It helps the service provider to spot any gaps or low performance, mainly in staff attitude, but also in terms of service delivery such as premises, cleanliness and more. Companies that are specialized in market research and service standards usually execute mystery shopping on behalf of the service providers. In general, freelancers conduct MYS. However, some authors[325] suggest that it should not be treated just as a freelancing job; it should be executed with passion, skill and commitment in a bid to measure the most important factors needed for the business's success. LDBs should adopt a MYS mechanism because they:[326]

1 evaluate the service and quality standards of the business;
2 identify weaknesses and problematic areas;
3 discover development potential;
4 provide benchmarking with competitors;
5 motivate the professional growth of employees;
6 reward the higher-performing employees.

According to Ipsos[327], the results of MYS are aggregated and used to identify and remedy systemic breakdowns of the desired and intended customer experience. When used effectively, MYS research can be a robust performance management tool that creates awareness of necessary standards, drives organizational behaviour change and ultimately leads to performance improvement and customer satisfaction. It is, however, crucial to structure and institutionalize the MYS mechanism into the LDB ecosystem in order to gain the maximum benefits. A proposed seven-step framework, which is based on the Ipsos approach that considers MYS as a standard research process that starts with a strategy and ends with an analysis of the gathered data, is shown in Figure 16.1.

Although this mechanism is widely practised in a range of industries across the world, mystery shopping lacks a generally approved theory and practice[328]. We nevertheless

FIGURE 16.1   Seven-step Mystery Shopping Approach

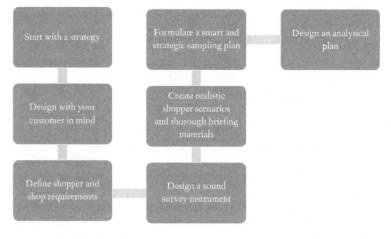

Source: Adapted from Ipsos report (2017)

advocate for this mechanism as an easily accessible and relatively cost-effective method that is geared towards learning about the strengths and areas for improvement in the vast majority of businesses. As will be discussed later in this chapter, several forms of MYS makes it an affordable and economical tool for gathering data and developing insights about business behaviour at various levels. We do, however, accept the fact that mystery shopping could be subjective and depends on the qualities of the shoppers and their level of training and objectivity. For example, when asked to note the number of 'smiling employees', shoppers have to apply their subjective judgement to assess how genuine the smile seems. The same applies to eye contact, courteousness, attention and helpfulness. Because mystery shopping is not a well-researched area, we decided to bring in opposing views as well, such as those of Blessing and Natter[329], who tested the relationship between MYS assessments, customer evaluations and sales performance with large-scale data from three retail service chains. They did not find a significant correlation. They therefore argued that mystery shoppers are not suitable substitutions for real customers. Clearly, then, the quality of the mystery shoppers is one of the critical success factors for effective MYS. Moreover, it is worth noting that a failure can happen if mystery shoppers are uncovered and spotted by the employees, because then all the investment in recruiting mystery shopping will be spent without the opportunity for any improvement.

We recommend further research into mystery shopping and invite contributions from industry leaders and practitioners around this mechanism.

Mystery shopping in action

To learn how guests view the organization, Mirage Aqua Park habitually benchmarks itself against data that has been collated by a customer service index and several other sources, including mystery shopping. To do this, they employ a company that specializes in market research and mystery shopping, which sends guests 'undercover' to evaluate the services provided in the park against predefined standards. In addition, the Business Excellence Department commissions individuals and families to run mystery shopping visits. Data collected from MYS events is shared with all employees through the Intranet and email notification system, once it has been subject to initial analysis, and every department is encouraged to offer their insights. To do this, every department confers internally and comes up with proposed actions based on contextualized data according to the departmental needs and targets. Outputs from all departments are then put together in a master list of proposed actions and changes and are sometimes submitted to the GM for approval, although in many cases, approval by the GM may not be required. In fact, for most of the cases, departmental managers and team leaders are empowered to act on the proposed actions. They also get access to finance according to a pre-set matrix of authority that is related to the size of expenditure for each job position. There is a monthly meeting dedicated to reviewing the effectiveness of the MYS practice; the members of these meetings are representatives from all departments.

'We also have a mystery guest running every quarter. We pass a checklist to the mystery guests on the area that we want them to focus on plus their general observations.' – Lana, guest relations officer, Mirage Aqua Park

The mystery shopping mechanism seems to be one of the dominant means of learning about competition. The management has found it useful, describing it as a 'major' source of learning that was applied in two ways: outbound and inbound. As an example of outbound learning, managers from Mirage Aqua Park practice mystery shopping at competitor organizations in order to compare and learn. Meanwhile inbound learning comes from the management recruiting its own mystery shoppers to visit their premises and evaluate their services, undercover. In the same manner, LAMAR Hotels & Resorts has developed five forms of mystery shopping, which are shown in Figure 16.2. These have been integrated with benchmarking. Two of these types are carried out at other organizations by LAMAR employees and managers to enable further learning from the competition, and three types are carried out inside the hotel to identify the potential areas for improvements.

The list of issues to be observed during such visits covers all lines of hotel service rather than specific services or outlets. At the end of the visit, a complete report is submitted to the executive committee so that they can explore the opportunities of adopting or adapting some or all of the observed approaches. Each visit covers more than one hotel in the same city.

FIGURE 16.2   Forms of Mystery Shopping at LAMAR Hotels & Resorts

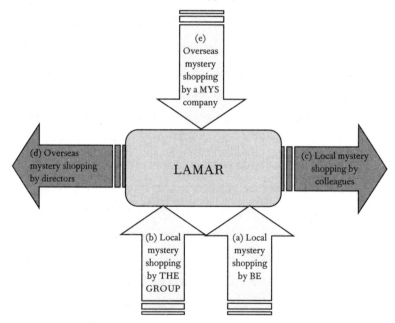

Source: Developed by the authors

The various forms are as follows:

a Local mystery shopping by Business Excellence (BE) at the hotel: in a newly introduced approach, the management decided to commission the Business Excellence Department to manage the mystery shopping for the entire organization and to recruit external professional local mystery shoppers to undertake this task;

b Local mystery shopping by The Group;

c Local mystery shopping by employees at competitors' venues: the managers and team leaders of the hotel regularly visit the websites of international five-star hotels in cities such as Tokyo, London, Singapore and New York to identify the traditional dishes offered and any new concepts in service. Some of these are adopted and, if considered worthwhile, such hotels are included in the next mystery guest visit to the city in question;

d Overseas mystery shopping by directors: for example, a team of four managers visited at least two other countries every six months to find out how luxury five-star hotels were being run there. They did this as mystery guests, i.e. the management of the hotel being visited was unaware of the purpose of their visit, and the team behaved like normal guests;

e Overseas mystery shopping by a third party: this form of mystery shopping is administered and executed by a third party – the specialist MYS company, which conducts such exercises only within the hospitality sector. According to the company statistics, its network of clients includes more than 967 hotels in various parts of the world. There is a perceived value addition through the implementation of this approach, which can be summarized in the following points:

+ Professional experts conducted the exercise with extensive experience in the hospitality sector;
+ The report produced by the MYS company compared LAMAR Hotels & Resorts against other hotels in the Middle East or other locations if preferred, making use of its access to the company Intranet. The anonymity of participating hotels is maintained.

The Business Excellence Department only facilitated the exercise – it was not conducted by BE staff themselves. Outside individuals were hired instead to act as hotel walk-in or overnight guests to evaluate the service by means of a checklist of predefined criteria. In this case, it was evident that a collective interpretation of information and ideas for improvement resulted from mystery shopping activities, and that these were discussed and reflected upon in order to identify learned lessons.

'We organize two visits every year to five-star hotels in several countries. We go to England, the USA, Singapore,

Hong Kong and Japan. We observe the process from A to Z. From the minute we leave the airport, we check the "meet and greet" in the car, because we book this service too, as we provide it here, so we want to see everything, from this very first step. We know what is in the car — water, drinks, newspapers, music, the courtesy of the driver etc. We stay at the hotel, but we visit other hotels to maximize the benefits of the visit. We eat in all the restaurants and use all their facilities. We order from the room as well, and sometimes we call from outside. We see what type of uniform their staff put on, the layout of the tables, the quality of the bedding, and the brand of cutlery they use, the number of towels in the bathrooms, the lotions, shampoo, and other stuff. At the end of the visit, we write a full in-depth report of everything we have seen on the visit. We come back, put this report on the table, and discuss all points to see which ones we can apply and which are irrelevant at this time. It is a massive exercise. Usually, three directors and managers accompany me. It is a good opportunity for managers to learn.' — Ricky, director, food and beverages, LAMAR Hotels & Resorts

Mystery shopping can combine two mechanisms: benchmarking and self-assessment. This may be considered a unique way of addressing the two OLPs, to which no reference was found in the literature we studied except for a few articles. We did find, however, an abundance of brief documents, mainly guidelines and codes of practice, which were available on the websites of professional bodies and some public authorities, especially in the UK and the US.

Learning from auditing

Similar to mystery shopping, auditing is an evaluation of performance against predefined criteria. However, it is not carried out undercover; audits can be spontaneous or pre-planned, but in both cases the identity of the professional auditor is known to the organization being audited. PWC[330] defines an audit as the examination of the financial report of an organization by someone who is independent of that organization. The American Society for Quality (ASQ)[331] defines auditing as an on-site verification activity, such as an inspection or examination, of a process or quality system, to ensure compliance to requirements.

Auditing is commonly associated with financial auditing, the purpose of which is to form a view on whether the information presented in the financial report, taken as a whole, reflects the financial position of the organization at a given date. In addition, there are various other types of audits, depending on which perspective we look at – for instance health and safety, risk, security, hygiene or culture. Furthermore, an audit can apply to an entire organization or might be specific to a specific function, process or production step. Some audits have particular administrative purposes, such as auditing documents, risk or performance, or following up on completed corrective actions. ISO 19011:2018[332] defines an audit as a 'systematic, independent and documented process for obtaining audit evidence and evaluating it objectively to determine the extent to which the audit criteria are fulfilled.

Proactive and preventive mechanisms

There is almost no documentation that explicitly associates learning with auditing, except for a few articles that argued that learning occurs when production experience results from generating audit reports, in which case this learning benefits only the auditors. Learning can be expanded by the audit team to complete the audit engagement and share the knowledge that has resulted from the audit activities. Walker[333], however, found out that auditors could be significant contributors to the level of organizational learning that occurs within regulatory programmes, as they help to enhance the compliance capability of firms and broaden enforcement options for regulators. We agree with the idea that auditors may be the ones who most benefit from the learning that occurs during the audit itself[334], but believe that this learning will be captured, and therefore transferred, into the audit reports about and for the business under audit. In a conventional business, the focus will be on closing any open non-conformities (i.e. the audit issues). In a LDB, however, the focus should also be on identifying the root cause of the non-conformity and putting measures in place to reduce or eliminate such issues in the future.

In addition to the above-mentioned types of audits, other classifications are internal and external. Internal audit is conducted by the business itself and in this way it is similar to self-assessment (see Chapter 12), whereas external audits are carried out by a third party, which could be a certification body, regulatory body or a customer. If a business has neither a self-assessment mechanism mindset nor a mechanism for internal review, the third-party audit or external audit may produce surprising findings and perhaps be viewed as a seeking out of failings and errors. This is an erroneous view. Audit should be deemed a positive experience, since it can be the best tool to determine if your business is as safe and compliant as it can and should be[335]. Furthermore, both internal and external audits can play a pivotal role in predicting errors and even disasters and can result in some of the most beneficial improvements to the business.

Take, for instance, the Deepwater Horizon disaster in 2010, when a blowout killed 11 workers and spewed 4 million barrels' worth of oil into the ocean for 87 days before it could be capped. This spillage devastated marine life and polluted 2,100km (1,300 miles) of shoreline. In addition, thousands were put out of work in the oil, fisheries and tourism industries[336]. The event prompted many questions, including: 'What if a proper risk and safety audit had been carried out, followed by appropriate actions?' Could this have saved lives and prevented such a disaster? This is an extreme case, but it just shows that in LDBs, risks need to be adequately assessed at every stage and the potential impact of a disaster measured, so that issues can be detected earlier.

How audits inform the LDB system

Audits can provide a complete 360-degree[337] view of the company and allow the management to understand the potential bottlenecks of a company well in advance. The auditing process helps in better decision-making by identifying issues and concerns, providing solutions and alternatives, enabling better planning, considering potential scenarios, detecting and reducing risk, and focusing on facts, which means that the management can adopt a factual approach to decision-making.

Summary

Although we could not find explicit suggestions that MYS is associated with organizational learning, it is assumed that when a service provider commissions a mystery shopper, there is a desire to spot the gaps in the service provision, extract the lessons learned and take action to fix the gaps. It can be considered either single-loop learning or double-loop learning based on the level of analysis that occurs. Similar to mystery shopping, auditing can play an instrumental role as a learning mechanism. However, it requires much effort to change the mindset and position auditing as a learning mechanism rather than a tool to identify errors and non-compliance. It is important to remember that in a LDB, audits should not be associated with any fear, as fear is a major barrier to learning.

Part Four

INTRODUCTION – LEARNING MEANS EXCELLENCE

It does not require much effort to prove that when organizations actively and proactively seek learning and invest in building and sustaining learning in all their activities, they transform into a Learning-Driven Business. This transformation into a LDB naturally leads to a focus on satisfying stakeholders and achieving critical organizational results, unleashing the potential of employees and realizing a vision. In the preceding three parts of this book, we discussed how learning could lead to better performance and sustained business, and why we firmly believe that learning means excellence. We built on empirical evidence and industry experience to conclude that LDBs have a much higher probability of achieving their objectives, and of reaching and sustaining excellence. Learning can assist organizations in their quest for continuous improvement by helping them to avoid the repetition of mistakes; by building sensitivity to the changing world so that the organization can adapt better; and by improving operations by understanding the weaknesses of the past and identifying how to correct them.

The literature in regard to LDB strongly suggests that OL and excellence can assist organizations in the quest for continuous improvement, from which the question emerges: Are OL and excellence two sides of the same coin? Our immediate answer is: yes. And others agree, as is evident from our research. Linking excellence to quality awards, Jacob et al[338] found that quality award winners are more successful firms and are valued more highly by investors. Others add caveats. For instance, Peters[339] argued that implementing effective total quality requires substantial investment in learning. According to Garvin[340], continuous improvement requires a commitment to learning: '...How, after all, can an organization improve without first learning something new?'.

What's more, McAdam et al[341] raised several questions related to the commonalities between OL and Total Quality (TQ)[342] that must be faced if progress is to be made in combining aspects of these fields. These questions are already being asked openly in organizations that have struggled to apply OL and TQ methods separately. For example: What are the underlying relationships between the approaches? An argument that arises from this question concerns the hierarchical order: Is TQ a subset of OL, or vice versa?

We believe it does not matter whether the approach is called Total Quality (TQ) or Organizational Learning (OL), simply because learning is woven into quality itself. There can be no quality without continuous improvement, and no continuous improvement without learning. There are also questions concerning differences and similarities: Are the differences in fact contradictions that cannot be reconciled? Does this result in organizational areas not being covered by either of the approaches? For Higan[343], though, organizational learning is an essential strategy that can be used by organizations to solve their problems, especially if they seek to also apply TQ.

17

The Learning-Driven Organization Model[344]

Introduction

In 2018, we presented the first version of the Learning-Driven Organization Model at the OLKC 2018 conference at Liverpool Business School. We received an abundance of feedback from researchers and practitioners, which we considered both in our paper that was published in 2019[345] and have drawn upon ever since. For instance, we stated that machine learning is a key mechanism in OL learning that can work across all levels. Indeed, as shown in Figure 17.1, machine learning overlaps all other mechanisms in the LDB. The LDO model remit answers three initial key questions, shown below, in addition to a more recent fourth one, which resulted from the major transformation after the advent of Industry 4.0 and Covid-19.

1 What makes an organization learning driven?
2 How and why does the learning ecosystem work organization wide?
3 How can we measure organizational learning?

4 How can organizations and governments survive and be sustainable in the Industry 4.0 and post-Covid-19 era.

To answer these, we have considered some of the key ideas relating to organizational learning, learning culture and measurement of the results of learning. In so doing, we have considered the development of an empirically based model of the Learning-Driven organization. The word 'ecosystem' is defined by *Oxford Dictionary* (2018) as 'a biological community of interacting organisms and their physical environment'. This is how organizations are behaving nowadays; we argue that organizations are ecosystems that have their own interacting dynamics on the one hand and on the other hand interact with their physical and virtual or digital environment. Learning is crucial to facilitate this ecosystem and help it to sustain and grow at the organizational level. In fact, the literature on organizational learning has emphasized its importance as critical for every organization[346]; moreover, there is a consensus that learning could be an organization's only source of sustainability[347].

There are a range of reasons why leaders and managers need to become learning driven. These include how much attention needs to be given to collaboration as well as to competition or whether adding benefit to communities and society in general needs to be given more prominence. This calls into question the extent to which the provision of learning will and should extend beyond organizational boundaries and bring some results to society overall.

We argue that learning was, has become and always will be *a critical process*. At a time when so many organizations, the people in those organizations and those who depend on organizations to live their lives are faced with many and often contradictory pressures, learning – by conscious human beings – needs to be pursued strategically, critically and become embedded in how we live and work.

Why an LDO model?

This LDO model is an attempt to provide leaders and practitioners in all circumstances and in any type of organization with an opportunity to become the drivers of learning. Based on a critical literature review and informed by primary and secondary data, we suggest that those organizations and those who make the essential decisions on how they work need to grasp a way of thinking and working that considers learning holistically and operationally and takes into account its impact beyond the boundaries of the operations. In the context of the LDO model, we define learning as: 'The process of modifying organizational behaviour through the use of different processes, practices, methods and activities in drawing lessons learned from within and outside the organization to improve performance and transform into a Learning-Driven organization systematically'. Our assumptions here are that learning remains primarily a feature of human existence. However, we must be aware that this might not always be the case; humans and non-humans taken together might one day become the unit for consideration[348].

Our LDO model is the outcome of 16 years of study to create meaning structures for organizational learning. Every day, people in organizations face problems of varying degrees of complication at all levels. While some problems can be easily solved, others defy quick resolution and can produce and reproduce conflicting interpretations of what is happening.

Understanding the nature and complexity of such problems requires a great deal of listening, understanding, reflection and analysis so that people can then find a way of moving forwards. This necessitates, therefore:

a the interpretations of the different people involved (including yourself);
b the various goals and expectations of those involved;
c a need to construct a way of proceeding.

In many cases, the way issues are framed locks people into a way of thinking and behaving, which might fix things in the short term but eventually brings back the original conditions of concern. In current times, we need learning to cope with exponential data and information overflow, and the new concepts and technologies that are evolving every day. We have already seen the development of things such as the gig economy, expert economy, Internet of things (IoT), Industry 4.0, smart cities, decision support systems (DSS), smart products, drones, digital medicine and so on, with more to come. In light of these advancements, it soon becomes clear that existing standards and frameworks cannot cope with the challenges; the major missing element throughout most existing frameworks and models is 'learning'. As we hope is clear by now, learning should be the core element of any standard.

Moreover, there is a significant need for a model that develops an ecosystem that helps organizations to shape their future. Until now, learning has mostly been 'caged' into literature and theory; even those leaders who claim to support learning do not always know where to start or how to sustain what they have begun. Fortunately, learning can be structured into a sustainable system that consists of a repository of good practices that can act as an eye-opener instead of a descriptive 'cookbook'.

The LDO model paints a picture of what learning may look like, making the intangible tangible by translating the theoretical frameworks and diverse learning theses into a language that people understand, digest and develop an enthusiasm for. This in turn enables them to act and transform knowledge into actions to feed and sustain an ecosystem for learning. As our society seems to enter rapidly into a new era of techno-humanism and dataism, it is obvious that there will be a pivotal need for a fast-learning approach to extract the lessons and package the takeaways.

For it is possible that unless mankind learns fast, and sets its direction, sooner or later artificial intelligence will prevail over consciousness[349].

Research methodology

The proposed LDO model builds on both primary and secondary empirical data collected from two case study organizations in the hospitality sector in Dubai, the UAE. The reason for selecting these two organizations was that both had been assessed against their organizational learning and overall performance within a National Quality Award context using the EFQM Excellence Model[350]. The assessment, which was organized by the Department of Economic Development in Dubai, was independent, external and undertaken by a team of voluntary assessors. Due to confidentiality concerns, the names of the organizations were not disclosed. Organization A employs 620 employees, and it achieved a high score in learning and excellence (685 / 1,000), while organization B employs 1,200 employees and achieved a low score of 285 / 1,000.

Organizational learning leads to performance improvement

In spite of the confusion about the meaning of OL, there was a consensus about its importance to the organizations' performance in the long term as well as the short term.

Authors such as Senge (1990) and many others[351] argue that learning is an important way to improve performance in the long term, and that in the near future, organizations that can utilize people's abilities, commitment and learning capacity in all levels can accomplish their goals and realize their vision. Put simply, organizations can improve their performances through OL. In order to confirm such claims about OL's importance, researchers have attempted to develop measures to see if and how its impact can indeed be measured objectively as well as based on judgements or opinions[352]. To measure OL, either we measure OL capabilities or OL processes. In addition, learning effects can be measured on an individual level, a team level and an organizational level[353]. Jyothibabu et al. (2010) attempted to develop a conceptual approach for measuring OL by merging the enablers' model[354] and the performance model[355]. That approach incorporated learning enablers, learning results (at individual, group and organizational level) and performance outcomes. However, it can be argued that individual learning levels (ILL), group learning levels (GLL) and organizational learning levels (OLL) can be considered as enablers as well as outcomes. Therefore, there is a need for a clearer approach for measurement that can focus on 'how to' undertake such measurement.

It is crucial to measure OL in order to assess its extent in organizations and understand how it supports the management of the organization[356]. One approach that is suggested is to measure the impact of OL based on errors and mistakes at work[357], yet this fails to take account of the context of the organizational climate. Indeed, most considerations of OL focus on one or two elements without taking a holistic approach. For example, some authors[358] focus on the ethos and philosophy that underpin OL, while others focus on individual and team learning cycles from a practice perspective[359] or on OL mechanisms and process[360]. Few authors focus on the measurement of OL[361]. Although all of the above areas of focus are indeed crucial for learning to occur and be sustained, learning does not occur due to culture or structure alone. For this reason, in our model we emphasize the need for an integrative ecosystem that incorporates three components of OL: culture, mechanisms and outcomes.

Organizational learning

Organizational learning (OL) has been and remains a source of interest among researchers and practitioners. Still, it is also a point of widespread controversy and confusion with regard to learning in or by organizations[362]. No single perspective in current learning theory is sufficient to capture fully the multiple connections and possibilities that learning creates and from which it emerges[363]. Nevertheless, as we stated earlier, it is claimed that OL has been a critical process ensuring the very existence of whole industries. Without OL, entirely new products and industries would not have been spawned[364]. Some authors[365], however, have been more sceptical about claims for OL and view the concept as an 'oxymoron' whereby learning can occur but can also be undermined by the processes of organizing. Learning and organizing, they say, can result in tensions that limit the potential of learning. Some have also been sceptical about the body of knowledge for OL as they think there appears to be more reviews of OL than there is substance to review. They therefore suggest addressing OL from a culture perspective.

Culture is defined by Cook and Yanow as a 'set of values, beliefs, and feelings, together with artefacts that are created, inherited, shared and transmitted within one group of people and that in part distinguish that group from others'[366]. Others define organizational culture as the relatively stable ways of perceiving the world and the action strategies that an organization has learned from experience[367]; therefore if the culture is rigid and strong enough to resist change then it will become dysfunctional. By contrast, if the culture is learning oriented, adaptive and flexible[368] then an organization can have perpetual learning. This implies that, as the culture changes, it may not be uniformly distributed throughout the organization; hence a mechanism may be required to establish and maintain the uniformity. Cue organizational learning culture (OLC), which is the culture that fosters the practices of acquisition of information, distribution and transfer of learning and recognition for learning-based application[369].

Culture and structures are two main conditions for organizational learning. If structures represent the relatively tangible 'hardware' of organizational learning, the organizational culture represent the 'software'[370]. In the same vein, Garvin[371] describes the organization that embraces and fosters a culture of learning as a learning organization, or 'an organization skilled at creating, acquiring, and transferring knowledge, and at modifying its behaviour to reflect new knowledge and insights'. OLC not only has a significant impact on creating organizational knowledge and on the overall organization's performance but it can also be a vital aspect of organizational culture and in effect form the core of a learning organization'[372]. A successful organization is an organization that considers learning as a success factor in business and is able to learn and integrate learning in its functions[373]. Fostering a learning culture will not only help employees to show high levels of performance but also will help to retain those employees in the organization[374]. They can also attract knowledgeable employees, enhance their level of commitment towards the organization[375] and reduce the employees' intention to leave the organization[376]. Having considered the plethora of literature on learning culture and its role in transforming organizations, we believe that OLC is the base of the Learning-Driven organization pyramid.

Leaders and managers can become Learning-Driven, but learning needs to be critical of assumptions made, the values that inform those assumptions and the consequences for what is done in practice. Because of this, it is essential to investigate learning processes within and beyond the traditional boundaries of an organization and how such processes can contribute towards 'organizational learning'.

Towards a Learning-Driven organization

Early advocates of OL provided little guidance on how to put organizational learning into practice in order to 'get there from here'[377]. A necessary condition for systematically promoting OL is the existence of OL structures in which the learning process can be carried out; the need to test organizational learning mechanisms can guide managerial actions towards reinforcing and fostering creativity[378]. Popper and Lipshitz's (1998, 2000) work is considered to be the first attempt to give clarity to the nature of organizational learning mechanisms (OLMs) as they provided the first comprehensive definition of these: 'institutionalized arrangements that allow organizations to systematically collect, analyse, store, retrieve and use information that is relevant to the performance of the organization and its members'[379].

Other authors[380] developed a theoretical framework of OLMs that classified three broad categories, namely cognitive, structural and procedural mechanisms, as follows:

a Cognitive mechanisms:
+ Clarity of strategy, connection strategy activities, coherence strategy training, learning
encouragement culture, and sharing of a common
language.
b Structural mechanisms:
+ Information between colleagues, knowledge
of who does what, participation in teamwork,
continuous improvement, and a framework for
seeking support.
c Procedural mechanisms:
+ Knowledge of resources and objectives, knowledge
of controlling criteria, midway reviews, post-
project reviews and routines regarding the use of
archives.

There is a pressing need for clarity and further classification
of OLMs as this will help organizations to construct
meanings from their learning practices and therefore will
enable the conversion of learning into strategies, policies
and procedures, i.e. to make OL more 'actionable'.

Organization-wide learning flow

As the links between individual learning and organization-
wide learning are instrumental for OL to occur, it is
necessary to understand the dynamics of such a relationship.
There are some instances when individual members of

an organization do not act, think or reflect on behalf of their organization, for instance where the organizational environment does not provide 'learning meadows'[381]. Therefore, when learning occurs and knowledge has been acquired, it stays in the individuals' minds rather than being diffused into the organization's fabric. In such cases, individuals become mere 'carriers of learning'[382]; in this case, the knowledge leaves when these carriers leave the organization. Building on this idea, organizational members in relation to their learning can be described as:

a Learning connectors:
   + Active members: learning agents who think, inquire, reflect and act on behalf of the organization.
b Learning incubators:
   + Members who acquire knowledge but are not able to bring it to the organization due to the absence of a system or complacency.
c Learning insulators:
   + Members who are disengaged and do not participate in learning activities.

For OL to occur, organizations need to encourage their members to act as learning connectors and should put measures in place and facilitate 'learning meadows' that bring learning incubators on board. They should also identify the learning insulators and put them on track by inquiring into the root cause of their attitudes and behaviours.

Organizational learning culture (why)

Without understanding organization culture, it becomes difficult to gain acceptance of change and to reap the benefit of what can be learned. Culture may be assessed and addressed though not limited to the following dimensions of practice for learning:

1.1 Leaders establish and nurture learning culture organization wide;
1.2 Leaders are role models for learning;
1.3 Trust is evident organization wide;
1.4 There is transparency and openness for learning;
1.5 Continuous improvement is embedded;
1.6 People are engaged at all levels;
1.7 Teamwork is encouraged and rewarded organization wide;
1.8 There is autonomy and empowerment in the decision-making process.

Organizational learning structure (how)

Organizational learning structure is defined by Friedman et al. (2001) as various learning processes, procedures and activities that are actively employed organization wide. This may include, but is not limited to, reflection, coaching, mentoring, after-action review, suggestions schemes and benchmarking:

OLM – policy level

2.1 There are various channels through which the organization can listen to its customers, partners and other stakeholders;

2.2 Feedback from all stakeholders is considered and acted upon;

2.3 Learning from others is encouraged and supported organization wide;

2.4 The organization participates in knowledge acquisition and dissemination activities outside the organization, nationally and internationally.

OLM – strategic level

2.5 Organization strategy sets a direction for learning and responds to the consequences;

2.6 Budget for organizational learning is secured and responsibility allocated;

2.7 Learning is articulated, shared, understood and implemented;

2.8 Learning needs are identified, acted upon and the outcome is measured for individuals, teams and organization wide;

2.9 Ongoing processes exist to consider the meaning of learning critically;

2.10 Learning outcomes are publicly acknowledged and published regularly;

2.11 Suggestions can flow into and within the organization, e.g. idea management systems, and internal blogs.

OLM – operational level

2.12 There are various types of activities to help people understand how they learn;

2.13 The organization is engaged in learning activities that extend beyond their previous boundaries;

2.14 Individuals and teams are recognized for learning;

2.15 Appropriate mechanisms such as coaching and mentoring are employed to engage and involve everyone at all organizational levels;

2.16 Lessons learned are documented, classified, communicated and utilized organization wide;

2.17 People at all levels have fair access to information that's appropriate to their needs;

2.18 People have fair access to support at all levels;

2.19 People are encouraged and supported to acquire further education and qualifications where applicable;

2.20 Appropriate technology is employed to support and facilitate learning.

Organizational learning outcomes (what)

Measurement enables the assessment of achievement. Measurement is crucial so that organizations can ascertain the extent to which the targeted results have been accomplished. Furthermore, measurement helps the assessment of the appropriateness of the employed learning mechanisms and approaches.

3.1 Learning is measured throughout the organization;

3.2 People are aware of how learning benefits them at their individual level and at the organization level;

3.3 Strategic and operational decisions are informed by learning outcomes, and the organization's leaders can give specific examples of strategic adaption;

3.4 Learning helps the organization to achieve its strategic objectives;

3.5 Employed learning mechanisms are reviewed so that the organization is fully aware of what works and what does not;

3.6 Learning enables the organization to innovate and develop or improve products and services;

3.7 Learning enables the organization to predict and shape its future.

Summary

The LDO model builds on the extensive contributions of the OL community of researchers and practitioners. It aims to highlight the importance of organizational learning further so that organizations and individuals know why they should invest in learning. It also helps organizations' management to have a roadmap that can guide them in their learning journey. Even though the positioning of the model seems to be influenced by normative language, as emphasized throughout the model, it is not meant to be a prescriptive 'cookbook' that may straightjacket organizations and individuals in their endeavour to learn. Rather, we hope the LDO model will help organizations to strategize learning.

18

Conclusion: The Way Forward

We call for learning to be the central focus of all organizations. We wish to see the Learning-Driven school, the Learning-Driven university, the Learning-Driven hospital, the Learning-Driven factory. We call for the Learning-Driven movement as we firmly believe that learning should go beyond business; it should be the critical focus of governments and societies, especially in the aftermath of the Covid-19 pandemic. Investing in learning and becoming Learning-Driven can no longer be optional.

Yet there remains the question of whether and to what extent our governments are organized and can learn and apply lessons to solve the significant governance challenges of our time and times to come[383]. Governance challenges such as climate change, financial crises, pandemics and leading and supporting fragile countries and economies are growing more complex, as is the knowledge required to solve them. There is also an increasing number of different stakeholders that need to be involved. Therefore, governments need to rethink the way they are organized so that they can learn from experiences and co-ordinate the process to meet these challenges. To address these problems, governments and societies need to pay more attention to learning, strategize learning and adopt learning mechanisms.

We live in a VUCA world[384]

VUCA is an acronym first used in 1987 and stands for volatility, uncertainty, complexity and ambiguity. It was used by the US Army War College in response to the collapse of the USSR in the early 1990s. Suddenly, there was no longer the singular enemy, meaning that new ways of seeing and reacting were required. The twenty-first century is branded by challenges that go beyond the problem-solving capabilities of individuals, organizations and single governments[385]. Increasingly, governments and societies face unprecedented rapid development of new technologies such as IoT, Industry 4.0 and AI, the growing diversity of political viewpoints and the increasing polarization of politics. As a result, the analysis of challenges and the process to find solutions and alternatives can become short-sighted, and lack the ability to foresight the future or at least to cope with the change.

When facing these local and global governance challenges, democratic governments around the world must find better ways to learn how best to provide public goods and services to their citizens – and thus reduce poverty, accelerate economic growth and improve sustainable development. Conventional wisdom and public opinion hold that governments do not learn from the past and that they make the same mistakes. However, there is a century-old tradition of pedagogical and organizational learning theories on the learning capacity of individuals and governments. Practitioners and scholars also agree that governments in both developed and developing countries are able and willing to learn from their past and other countries' experiences if they build the capacity to do so[386]. It is hoped that learning and wisdom will prevail in the world, and no one will be left behind. Hence we will be able to solve our problems, survive and grow.

What if we fail to learn or action what we learned?

Apart from primary benchmarking data or 'what works' studies, not much is documented about how governments learn best or what exactly makes them change their behaviour in a targeted way to solve the governance challenges they face. Governmental learning can be complex and hard to conceptualize since it must address many cultural, political, religious and social particularities, psychological barriers and practical constraints that might hinder or even prevent learning at all. While governmental learning thus appears challenging to understand and to initiate, there are encouraging empirical examples and theoretical concepts that provide hope. But what if we fail to learn or fail to enact learning? This is an unsafe scenario, which will sooner or later lead to more disasters and more pernicious and perhaps insurmountable problems. If this is the case, the world will not be a safe or suitable place in which to live, which is surely a scenario that no one wishes to witness. We are keen to hear your views on this, and all matters related to the LDB. You are welcome to share your thoughts at www.learningdrivenbusiness.com

A final word

Strategic learning is about understanding a global strategy and how each business unit in an organization contributes its best, most innovative thinking, followed by actions that execute the strategic intent of the organization. We believe that strategic learning is the most effective and sustainable approach in helping organizations to reach their strategic objectives. In conclusion, if achieving strategic objectives is important to organizations, they need to strategize learning, and to do this they need to become Learning-Driven organizations.

REFERENCES

1   http://qfd-institute.blogspot.com/2012/07/learning-is-not-compulsory-neither-is.html (Accessed 8 June 2020)

2   https://olc.worldbank.org/content/about-olc (Accessed 12 November 2019).

3   Easterby-Smith, MPV & Araujo, LM 1999, 'Organizational learning: current debates and opportunities'. In M Easterby-Smith, L Araujo & J Burgoyne (eds), *Organizational Learning and the Learning Organization: Developments in Theory and Practice*. Sage, London, pp. 1-21.

4   Sambrook, S. (2002) 'Factors Influencing Learning in Work: A comparison of two research projects' (European and United Kingdom-based), *European Educational Research Journal*, Vol.1, No. 3, p. 533.

5   DiBella, A. & Nevis, E. (1998) *How Organizations Learn: An Integrated Strategy for Building Learning Capability*. San Francisco: Jossey-Bass.

6   Brockbank, A., McGill, I., and Beech, N., (Eds.) (2002), *Reflective Learning in Practice*, Gower, England.

7   Learning Declaration Group (2000) A Declaration on Learning: A Call to Action. p. 7. Retrieved from URL = https://files.eric.ed.gov/fulltext/ED492408.pdf (Accessed on 20 April 2019)

8   https://www.bbc.co.uk/news/technology-52340651 (Accessed 5 May 2020).

9   Anuradha, T. and Sujatha, D. (2019). 'Role of strategic leader in the VUCA world'. *International Journal of Advance and Innovative Research*, Volume 6, Issue 1, pp. 72–76.

10 Alvesson, M. and Spicer, A. (2012). 'A Stupidity-Based Theory of Organizations'. *Journal Of Management Studies*, 49(7), pp. 1194–1220.

11 https://www.thehubrishub.com/ (Accessed 5 January 2020).

12 Zaleznick, A. (1977). 'Leaders and managers: are they different?'. *Harvard Business Review*, September/October: 67–78; Kotter, J.P. (1990). 'A Force for Change: How Leadership Differs from Management', Free Press.

See also Bratton, J. (2020). *Organizational Leadership*, Sage for a recent consideration of leadership theories, models, ideas and training.

13 Avolio, B., and Bass, B. (2004). *Multifactor Leadership Questionnaire: Manual and Sampler Set*, Mind Garden. Retrieved from http://www.mindgarden.com/documents/MLQGermanPsychometric.pdf (Accessed 15 October 2020)

14 Dinh, J., Lord, R.G., Gardner, W., Meuser, J.D., Liden, R., and Hu, J. (2014). 'Leadership Theory and Research in the New Millennium: Current Theoretical Trends and Changing Perspectives'. *The Leadership Quarterly* 25, pp. 36–62.

15 Knippenberg, D. V., and Sitkin, S. B. (2013). 'A Critical Assessment of Charismatic—Transformational Leadership Research: Back to the Drawing Board?' *The Academy of Management Annals*, 7(1)., pp. 1–60.

16 Thomas, J. B., Sussman, S. W., Henderson, J. C. (2001). 'Understanding "Strategic Learning": Linking Organizational Learning, Knowledge Management, and Sensemaking'. *Organization Science* 12(3), pp. 331–345.

17 Board, D. (2010). 'Leadership: The ghost at the trillion dollar crash?'. *European Management Journal*, 28(4), pp. 269–277.

18 Adapted from Mingers, J. (2000). '"What is it to be critical?" Teaching a critical approach to management undergraduates'. *Management Learning*, Vol. 31, No.2, pp. 219–37, and Antonacopoulou, E. P. (2004). 'Introducing Reflexive Critique in the Business Curriculum Reflections on the Lessons Learned'. Advanced Institute of Management.

19 Bolden, R., Hawkins, B., Gosling, J., and Taylor, S. (2011). *Exploring Leadership: Individual, Organizational, and Societal Perspectives*, Oxford University Press.

20 https://www.equalitytrust.org.uk/scale-economic-inequality-uk for details of high income inequality in the UK. (Accessed 17 June 2020).

21 Kelly, S. (2014). 'Towards a negative ontology of leadership', *Human Relations*, Vol. 67(8), pp. 905–922.

22 Gronn, P. (2009). 'Leadership Configurations'. *Leadership*, 5(3), pp. 381–394.

23 Mintzberg, H. (1987). 'Crafting strategy'. *Harvard Business Review*, July/August, pp. 66–75.

24 Mintzberg, H., Ahlstrand, B. and Lampel, J. (1998). *Strategy Safari*, Prentice Hall.

25 Micheli, P., and Manzoni, J-F. (2010). 'Strategic Performance Measurement: Benefits, Limitations and Paradoxes'. *Long Range Planning* 43, pp. 465–476.

26 https://www.cgma.org/resources/tools/essential-tools/strategic-planning-tools.html (Accessed 18 March 2020) for a consideration of different strategic planning tools.

27 Jarzabkowski, P. (2008). 'Shaping strategy as a structuration process'. *Academy of Management Journal* Vol. 51, No. 4, pp. 621–650.

28 Mooney, T., and Brinkerhoff, R. O. (2008). *Courageous Training*, San Francisco, Berrett-Koehler for a key explanation of the importance of business strategy for learning in organizations.

29 Goldman, E. F., Scott, A. R., and Follman, J. M. (2015). 'Organizational practices to develop strategic thinking'. *Journal of Strategy and Management*, Vol. 8 No. 2, pp. 155–175.

30 We have adapted these words from a famous psychologist, John Shotter, who died in 2016.

31 Sammut-Bonnici, T. (2014). 'Strategic drift'. In Cooper C. (Ed.) *Wiley Encyclopedia of Management*, John Wiley and Sons. Retrieved from https://www.um.edu.mt/library/oar/bitstream/123456789/21864/1/sammut-bonnici%20strategic%20drift.pdf (Accessed 14 October 2020)

32 Barabba V. P., and Mitroff, I. I. (2014). 'Assumptions—Strategic Assumption Surfacing and Testing (SAST)' in *Business Strategies for a Messy World: Tools for Systemic Problem-Solving*, Palgrave Pivot, pp. 22–34.

33 Di Stefano, G., Gino, F., Pisano, G. P., and Staats, B. R. (2014). 'Making Experience Count: The Role of Reflection in Individual Learning', https://doi.org/10.2139/ssrn.2414478

34 Ortenblad, A. (2004). 'The Learning Organization: Towards an Integrated Model', *The Learning Organization*, Vol. 11, No. 2, pp. 129–144.
Mitki, Y. et al. (1997). 'Organizational learning mechanisms and continuous improvement: A longitudinal study', *Journal of Organizational Change Management*, Vol. 10, No. 5, pp. 426–446.
Argyris, C., and Schon, D. (1996). *Organizational Learning II: Theory, method and practice*, Addison Wesley, pp. 20–33.

35 Brockbank, A., McGill, I., and Beech, N., (Ed.) (2002), *Reflective Learning in Practice*, Gower, p6.

36 Ibid.

37 Burgoyne, J., and Reynolds, M. (1997). *Management Learning: Integrated perspective in theory and practice*, Sage, pp. 1–3.

38 Schön, D. (2016). *The reflective practitioner : how professionals think in action.* Routledge.

39 https://content.iriss.org.uk/reflectivepractice/practitioner.html

40 Argyris, C., and Schon, D. (1996). *Organizational Learning II: Theory, method and practice.*, Addison Wesley.

41 Ibid, p.20

42 Siebert, K. W., and Daudelin, M. D. (1999). *The role of reflection in management learning: theory, research and practice*, Quorum, p. 4.

43 Ibid, p.3

44 Kolb, D. A. (2014). *Experiential Learning: Experience as the Source of Learning and Development*, FT Press.

45 Gold, J., and Holman, D. (2001). 'Let me tell you a story: an evaluation of the use of storytelling and argument analysis in management education'. *Career Development International* 6/7, pp. 384–395.

46 Argyris, C., and Schon, D. (1996). *Organizational Learning II: Theory, method and practice*, Addison Wesley.

47 Chris Argyris made a crucial contribution to organizational learning. He highlighted how organizations and people can present or espouse what they want to do but act differently. He also explained how theories-in-use can differ from what they espouse. See Argyris, C. (1976). 'Theories of action that inhibit individual learning'. *American Psychologist*, vol. 31, no. 9, pp. 638–54.

48 https://www.hrzone.com/profile/kliebenguth (Accessed 8 June 2020).

49 Lane, P. J., Koka, B. R., and Pathak, S. (2006). 'The reification of absorptive capacity: a critical review and rejuvenation of the construct'. *Academy of Management Review*, Vol., 31, No. 4, pp. 833–863.

50 Mezirow. J. (1990). *Fostering Critical Reflection*. Jossey-Bass and https://www.instructionaldesign.org/theories/transformative-learning/ (Accessed 17 March 2020).

51 Toulmin, S. (1958). *The Uses of Argument*, Cambridge University Press and https://owl.purdue.edu/owl/general_writing/academic_writing/historical_perspectives_on_argumentation/toulmin_argument.html (Accessed 10 December 2019) for a detailed example of the Toulmin's box diagram.

52 An interview with Oprah Winfrey on WCVB-TV 5 News *CityLine* (13 January 2002). Cited in https://sites.sph.harvard.edu/wmy/celebrities/ (Accessed 11 June 2020).

53 Chapathes, M. R., (2006) 'Coaching for Performance Improvement: The COACH model'. *Development and Learning Organization*, Vol. 20, No. 2, pp. 17–18.

54 Gregson, K. (1993), 'Mentoring'. *Work Study*, Vol. 42, No. 6, pp. 19–20.

55 https://www.cipd.co.uk/Images/west-yorkshire-mentoring-pack_2011_tcm18-9423.pdf (Accessed 17 May 2020).

56 https://www.inc.com/john-rampton/10-reasons-why-a-mentor-is-a-must.html (Accessed 19 May 2020).

57 Clutterbuck, D., (2008). 'What's happening in coaching and mentoring? And what is the difference between them?'. *Development and Learning in Organizations*, Vol. 22, No. 4, pp. 8–10.

58   Blackman-Sheppard, G., (2004). 'Executive Coaching'. *Industrial and Commercial Training*, Vol. 36, No. 1, pp. 5–8.

59   Ibid.

60   Emelo, R. (2009). 'Mentoring in tough times', *Industrial and commercial Training*, Vol. 41, No. 4, pp. 207–211.

61   https://www.mentoring.org/new-site/wp-content/uploads/2019/12/ E-Mentoring-Supplement-to-EEP-1.pdf (Accessed 11 July 2020).

62   http://ecomentor.ios.edu.pl/images/Materialypromocyjne/ Newsletter_1/EcoMentor_Mentoring-in-Industry-4.0.pdf (Accessed 13 April 2020).

63   See a list of online mentoring platforms at https://www.growthmentor.com/ blog/online-mentoring-platforms-software/ (Accessed 15 April 2020).

64   Parsloe, E. (1999). *The Manager as Coach and Mentor*, McGraw-Hill Education / Europe, Middle East & Africa, p. 8.

65   https://dictionary.cambridge.org/us/dictionary/english/coaching (Accessed 11 February 2020).

66   https://mentoringgroup.com/what-is-coaching.html (Accessed 20 February 2020).

67   Case, T. J, and Kleiner, B. H, (1993). 'Effective Coaching of Organizational Employees', *Work Study*, Vol. 42, No. 3, pp. 7–10.

68   Bowerman, J., and Collins, G., (1999). 'The coaching network: a programme for individual and organizational development'. *Journal of Workplace Learning: Employee counselling today*, Vol. 11, No. 8, pp. 191–197.

69   Drake, D. B. (2007). 'The art of thinking narratively: Implications for coaching psychology and practice', *Australian Psychologist*, 42(4), pp. 283–294.

70   https://www.westyorkshire.police.uk/sites/default/files/files/reports/ west_yorkshire_police_-_staff_survey_report_-_issued_30_march_2016. pdf (Accessed 25 October 2020) for the results of a survey completed two years after a negative report in 2014.

71   Hooijberg, R., Hunt, J. G., Antonakis, J., Boal, K. B., and Lane, N. (2007). *Monographs in Leadership and Management, Volume 4: Being there even when you are not: leading through strategy, structures, and systems*. Bingley: Emerald Group Publishing Limited, pp. 375–408.

72   Ibarra, H., and Scoular, A. (2019). 'The leader as coach'. *Harvard Business Review*, November-December, pp. 111–119.

73   Bierema, L. L., and Hill, J. R. (2005). 'Virtual mentoring and HRD', *Advances in Developing Human Resources*, 7(4), pp. 556–568.

74   Yurkschatt, J. (2015). 'Importance of Cross Training in the Workplace', available at https://www.directrecruiters.com/career-advice-2/importance-of-cross-training-in-the-workplace/ (Accessed 30 May 2020).

75 Williams, L. (2019) 'An Overview of Cross-Training', available at https://www.verywellfit.com/crosstraining-4157104 (Accessed 12 February 2020).

76 Baverstock, J. (2019). 'What is cross training?'. *Nuffield Health*, available at https://www.nuffieldhealth.com/article/what-is-cross-training (Accessed 10 February 2020).

77 Yurkschatt, J. (2015). 'Importance of Cross Training in the Workplace'. Available at https://www.directrecruiters.com/career-advice-2/importance-of-cross-training-in-the-workplace/ (Accessed 30 May 2020).

78 Abrams, C., and Berge, Z. (2010). 'Workforce cross training: a re-emerging trend in tough times'. *Journal of Workplace Learning*, Vol. 22, No. 8, pp. 522–529, available at https://doi.org/10.1108/13665621011082882 (Accessed: 12 March 2020).

79 https://gbq.com/why-cross-training-your-accounting-staff-is-key/ (Accessed: 28 June 2020).

80 'Adapting workplace learning in the time of coronavirus'. Available at https://www.mckinsey.com/business-functions/mckinsey-accelerate/our-insights/adapting-workplace-learning-in-the-time-of-coronavirus (Accessed 29 June 2020).

81 Salem, S. E. and Abdien, M. K. (2017). 'Implementation of employee cross-training during perilous conditions in hotels'. *Tourism Management Perspectives*, Vol. 23, pp. 68–74, ISSN 2211-9736, https://doi.org/10.1016/j.tmp.2017.05.005 (Accessed: 19 June 2020).

82 Stanica, S. and Peydro, J. (2016). 'How does the employee cross-training lean tool affect the knowledge transfer in product development processes?', VINE Journal of Information and Knowledge Management Systems, Vol. 46, No. 3, pp. 371–385, available at https://doi.org/10.1108/VJIKMS-11-2015-0061 (Accessed: 5 March 2020).

83 Salehi, F., and Yaghtin, A. (2015). 'Action research innovation cycle: lean thinking as a transformational system'. *Procedia – Social and Behavioral Sciences*, Vol. 181, pp. 293–302.

84 Beleich. C. (2020). '6 Major Benefits To Cross-Training Employees', available at https://www.edgepointlearning.com/blog/cross-training-employees/ (Accessed 27 June 2020).

85 Asselta, C., and Sperl, C. (2020). 'Cross Training: Value in Today's Environment'. Akziom Consulting website, available at http://www.akziom.com/yahoo_site_admin/assets/docs/Cross_Training.302190448.pdf (Accessed 25 June 2020).

86 Internal document (n.d), 'Cross Training Guide, Training Manual (The Group)'. pp. 3–4.

87   'Cross-skilling training to support medical redeployment in the Covid-19 pandemic'. Available from https://www.rcpjournals.org/content/futurehosp/early/2020/05/22/fhj.2020-0049.full.pdf (Accessed 29 June 2020).

88   For further resources and providing feedback, visit the book website at http://www.learningdrivenbusiness.com (Accessed: 20 October 2020).

89   Senge, P. M. (1990). *The Fifth Discipline: the Art and Practice of the Learning Organization*, Doubleday/Currency.

90   Garad, A. and Gold, J. (2019). 'The learning-driven organization: toward an integrative model for Organizational learning'. *Industrial and Commercial Training*, Vol. 51, No. 6, pp. 329–341, available at https://doi.org/10.1108/ICT-10-2018-0090 (Accessed: 22 July 2020).

91   Salas, E., Dickinson, T. L., Converse, S. A., and Tannenbaum, S. I. (1992). 'Toward an understanding of team performance and training,' in *Teams: Their Training and Performance*, eds R. W. Swezey and E. Salas (Westport, CT: Ablex Publishing), pp. 3–29.

92   Edmondson, A. C., Dillon, J. R., and Roloff, K. S. (2007). 'Three perspectives on team learning: outcome improvement, task mastery, and group process'. *Acad. Manage. Ann.* 1, pp. 269–314. DOI 10.1080/078559811 (Accessed 16 July 2020).

93   Sarin, S., and McDermott, C. (2003). 'The effect of team leader characteristics on learning, knowledge application, and performance of cross-functional new product development teams'. *Decis. Sci. 34*, pp. 707–739. DOI 10.1111/j.1540-5414.2003.02350.x (Accessed 6 June 2020).

94   Edmondson, A. (1999). 'Psychological safety and learning behavior in work teams', *Adm. Sci. Q. 44*, pp. 350–383. DOI 10.2307/2666999 (Accessed 17 July 2020).

95   Wiese, C. W., and Burke, C. S. (2019). 'Understanding Team Learning Dynamics Over Time', *Front. Psychol.* 10:1417. DOI 10.3389/fpsyg.2019.01417, available at https://www.frontiersin.org/articles/10.3389/fpsyg.2019.01417/full (Accessed 1 July 2020).

96   Wong, S.-S. (2004). 'Distal and local group learning: performance trade-offs and tensions', *Organ. Sci.* 15, pp. 645–656. DOI 10.1287/orsc.1040.0080 (Accessed: 30 May 2020).

97   Wilson, J. M., Goodman, P. S., and Cronin, M. A. (2007). 'Group learning', *Acad. Manage. Rev.* 32, pp. 1041–1059. DOI 10.2307/20159355 (Accessed: 14 May 2020).

98   Senge, P. (2001). *From Post-Mortem to Living Practice: An In-Depth Study of the Evolution of the After Action Review.* (Accessed 21 October 2020)

99   https://www.britannica.com/event/Hurricane-Katrina (Accessed: 22 March 2020).

100 Report can be retrieved from https://www.hsdl.org/?view&did= 31248 (Accessed: 12 December 2019).

101 https://improvement.nhs.uk/documents/2087/after-action-review.pdf (Accessed: 9 November 2019).

102 EFQM, (2005). 'The EFQM Framework for Knowledge Management'. EFQM, p. 36.

103 Lipshitz, R., Friedman, V. J. and Popper, M. (2007). *Demystifying Organizational Learning*, Sage Publications.

104 TC 25-20 (1993). 'A Leader's Guide to After-Action Review, A Training Circular'. US Army available at https://www.acq.osd.mil/dpap/ccap/ cc/jcchb/Files/Topical/After_Action_Report/resources/tc25-20.pdf (Accessed: 5 January 2020).

105 Adapted from TC 25-20 (1993, p. 5).

106 Townsend, P. L., and Gebhardt, J. E, (2007), *How Organizations Learn: Investigate, Identify, Institutionalise*, ASQ Quality Press.

107 Garvin, D. (2000), *Learning in Action: A guide to putting the Learning Organizations to work*, Harvard Business School Press, p. 48.

108 Darling, M., Parry, C., and Moore, J. (2005), *Learning in the Thick of it*, Harvard Business Review, July–August, 2005, retrieved from https://hbr. org/2005/07/learning-in-the-thick-of-it (Accessed 20 May 2020).

109 Training available at https://portal.e-lfh.org.uk/Component/Details/ 536402

110 For a short read about AARs in project environments, see https://www. mindtools.com/pages/article/newPPM_73.htm (Accessed 30 November 2019).

111 EFQM (2005). 'The EFQM Framework for Knowledge Management'. EFQM, p. 36.

112 Senge, P. M. (1990). *The Fifth Discipline: the Art and Practice of Learning Organizations*, Random House.

113 https://usaidlearninglab.org/sites/default/files/resource/files/ afteractionreviewguidancemarch2013.pdf

114 Townsend, P. L., and Gebhardt, J. E, (2007). *How Organizations Learn: Investigate, Identify, Institutionalise*, ASQ Quality Press.

115 More AARs examples can be found at https://thesystemsthinker.com/ emergent-learning-in-action-the-after-action-review/ (Accessed 10 July 2020).

116 https://www.conovercompany.com/teamwork-solving-problems/ (Accessed 6 April 2020).

117 Marks, M. A., Mathieu, J. E., and Zaccaro, S. J. (2001). 'A temporally based framework and taxonomy of team processes'. *Academy of Management* Rev. 26, pp. 356–376. DOI 10.2307/259182 (Accessed 6 October 2019).

118 Jones, L. N., and McBride, L. C., (1990). *An Introduction to Team-approach problem Solving* ASQC, Quality Press (Accessed 8 May 2020).

119 Argyris, C., and Schon, D. (1996). *Organizational Learning II: Theory, method and practice*, Addison Wesley.

120 Tucker, A. L., Edmondson, E., and Spear, S., (2002) 'When problem solving prevents organizational learning'. *Journal of Organizational Management Change*, Vol. 15, No. 2, pp. 122–137.

121 Seta, K., Tachibana, K., Fujisawa, I., and Umano, M. (2004). 'An ontological approach to interactive navigation for problem solving oriented learning processes'. *Interactive Technology and Smart Education*, Vol. 1, No. 3, pp. 185–193.

122 Cooke, D. L., and Rohleder, T. R., (2006). 'Learning from incidents: from normal accidents to high reliability'. *System Dynamics Review*, Vol. 22, No.3, pp. 213–239.

123 Argyris, C. (1991). 'Teaching Smart People How to Learn'. *Harvard Business Review* May–June, pp. 99–109 (and cited in Seibert and Daudelin, 1999).

124 Original management thinker Reg Revans (14 May 1907–8 January 2003) developed the action learning concept in the 1940s. His extraordinary 95 years encompassed many successful achievements, from competing in the Olympics, working as an astrophysicist, educational administrator and university professor to the culmination of his career as an international management consultant. https://www.actionlearningassociates.co.uk/ action-learning/reg-revans/ (Accessed 2 July 2020).

125 Mumford, A., (1991). 'Individual and Organizational Learning: in the pursuit of change'. *Industrial and Commercial Training*, Vol. 23 No. 6, pp. 24–31.

126 Tucker, A. L., Edmondson, E., and Spear, S., (2002). 'When problem solving prevents organizational learning'. *Journal of Organizational Management Change*, Vol. 15, No. 2, pp. 122–137.

127 Garvin, D. (2000). *Learning in Action: A guide to putting the Learning Organizations to work*, Harvard Business School Press.

128 Dixon N. M. (2017). *The Organizational Learning Cycle: How we can learn collectively*, Gower.

129 Argyris, C., and Schon, D. (1996). *Organizational Learning II: Theory, method and practice*, Addison Wesley.

130 Seta, K., Tachibana, K., Fujisawa, I., and Umano, M. (2004). 'An ontological approach to interactive navigation for problem solving oriented learning processes'. *Interactive Technology and Smart Education*, Vol. 1, No. 3, pp. 185–193.

131 https://www.kaizen.com/

132 INTRAC (2020), 'Action Learning Sets: A Guide for Small and Diaspora NGOs' available at https://www.intrac.org/wpcms/wp-content/uploads/2016/09/Action-Learning-Sets-An-INTRAC-guide-1.pdf (Accessed 16 May 2020).

133 Pedler, M. (1996/2008) *Action Learning for Managers*, Gower.

134 In the UK, coal mines were nationalized in 1946, and privatized in the 1990s.

135 Dickenson, M., Burgoyne, J., and Pedler, M. (2010). 'Virtual action learning: practices and challenges', *Action Learning Research and Practice*, 7(1) pp. 59–72.

136 Vince, R. (2004). 'Action Learning and organizational learning; power, politics and emotion in organizations'. *Action Learning, Research and Practice*, Vol.1. pp. 63–68.

137 Revans, R. (1982). *The Origins and Growth of Action Learning*, Chartwell-Bratt.

138 Boshyk, Y. (2016). *Business Driven Action Learning*, Springer.

139 Anderson, L., and Coleman, C. (2014) 'Action learning: approaches, applications and outcomes' in Kraiger, K., Passmore, J., Rebelos dos Santos, N., and Malvezzi, S. (eds). *The Wiley Blackwell Handbook of the Psychology of Training, Development, and Performance Improvement*, Wiley-Blackwell.

140 Rigg, C., and Trehan, K. (2004). 'Reflections on working with critical action learning'. *Action Learning: Research and Practice*, Vol. 1, No. 2, pp. 149–165.

141 Gold, J. (2014). 'Revans reversed: focusing on the positive for a change'. *Action Learning: Research and Practice*. DOI 10.1080/14767333.2014.936927 (Accessed 4 July 2020).

142 Cooperrider, D. L., and Whitney, D. (2000). 'A Positive Revolution in Change.' In Golemiewwski R. T. (Ed.) *Handbook of Organizational Behavior*, Marcel Decker, pp. 611–629.

143 Devins, D., Gold, J., and Boak, G. (2020). 'Action Learning and Action Research to Alleviate Poverty'. *Action Learning: research and practice*, 17(1), pp. 48–61.

144 NHS (2008). 'Skills for Success'. available at https://www.libraryservices.nhs.uk/document_uploads/Staff_Development/nlh_sdg_introducing_learning_sets_200808.pdf (Accessed 1 June 2019).

145 FAO (2020). Available at http://www.fao.org/elearning/course/FK/en/pdf/trainerresources/PG_ALSets.pdf (Accessed 3 April 2020).

146 Casey, D. (1996). *Managing Learning in Organizations*, Open University Press.

147 Castka, P., Bamber, C. J., Sharp, J. M., and Belohoubek, P. (2001). 'Factors affecting successful implementation of high performance teams'. *Team Performance Management*, Vol. 7, Nos. 7/8, pp. 123–134.

148 Nonaka, I., and Takeuchi, H. (1996). *The Knowledge Creating Company*, Oxford University Press.

149 Senge, P. M. (2010). *The Fifth Discipline: the Art and Practice of Learning Organizations*, Penguin Random House.

150 Scholtes, P., Joiner, B., and Streibel, B. (1996) *The Team Handbook*, Oriel.

151 Hill, F. M. (1996). 'Organizational Learning for TQM through quality circles'. *TQM Magazine*, Vol. 8, No. 6, pp. 53–57.

152 Casey, D. (1996). *Managing Learning in Organizations*, Open University Press.

153 For a list of retail businesses that closed or were facing difficulty in 2019–20, go to https://www.retailresearch.org/whos-gone-bust-retail.html#bycompany (Accessed 11 June 2020).

154 The *Guardian* (25 May 2020), available at https://www.theguardian.com/fashion/2020/may/25/shopping-habits-of-generation-z-could-spell-end-of-fast-fashion (Accessed 4 June 2020).

155 Bell, W. (2001). 'Futures studies comes of age: twenty five years after the limits to growth'. *Futures*, 33(1), pp. 63–76.

156 Son, H. (2015). 'The history of Western futures studies: An exploration of the intellectual traditions and three-phase periodization', *Futures*, 66, pp. 120–137.

157 Glenn, J. C. (2009). 'Introduction to the futures research methods series' *Futures Research Methodology*, The American Council for the United Nations University (The Millennium Project, Introduction Chapter. Available on CD-ROM format.

158 Micic, P. (2010). *The Five Futures Glasses*, Palgrave.

159 Bell, W. (1997). 'The purposes of futures studies'. *The Futurist*, Nov–Dec, pp. 42–45.

160 Wilkinson, A., and Ramirez, R. (2010). 'Canaries in the Mind: Exploring How the Financial Crisis Impacts 21st Century Future-Mindfulness'. *Journal of Futures Studies* 14(3): pp. 45–60.

161 Gordon, T. J., and Todorova, M. (2019). *Future Studies and Counterfactual Analysis: Seeds of the Future*, Palgrave.

162 https://smallbusiness.chron.com/reason-use-swot-pestle-analysis-40810.html (Accessed 27 April 2020) for further details of these methods.

163 Cuhls, K. E. (2019). 'Horizon Scanning in Foresight – Why Horizon Scanning is only a part of the game'. *Futures and Foresight Science*, 2(7), pp. 1–21 https://www.researchgate.net/publication/337488949_Horizon_Scanning_in_Foresight_-_Why_Horizon_Scanning_is_only_a_part_of_the_game (Accessed 22 October 2020)

164 https://scholar.google.com/ (Accessed 12 April 2020).

165 The different method can be considered by going to https://www.gov.uk/government/publications/futures-toolkit-for-policy-makers-and-analysts

(Accessed 18 August 2020) where there is a free toolkit available to explain the methods.

166 Bishop, P., Hines, A., and Collins, T. (2007). 'The current state of scenario development: An overview of techniques', *Foresight*, 9(1), pp. 5–25.

167 Van der Heijden, K. (1996). *Scenarios: The art of strategic conversation*, John Wiley & Sons.

168 Since the 1970s, Shell has been developing the scenario as a method and you can find examples of this at their website. Go to https://www.shell.com/energy-and-innovation/the-energy-future/scenarios.html (Accessed 9 July 2020) where you can also download some of their current work, such as the digitalization of society at https://www.shell.com/energy-and-innovation/the-energy-future/scenarios/scenario-sketches/sketch-the-digitalisation-of-society/_jcr_content/par/relatedtopics.stream/1580996487973/055348b123693dd5cf3a52debfb1f43cd15e506b/scenarios-dos-websummit-digital-essay.pdf

169 Micic, P. (2010). *The Five Futures Glasses*, Palgrave.

170 Curry, A., and Schultz, W. (2009). 'Roads Less Travelled: Different Methods, Different Futures', *Journal of Futures Studies*, 13(4), pp. 35–60.

171 Hines, A., and Gold, J. (2015). 'An organizational futurist role for integrating foresight into corporations'. *Technological Forecasting and Social Change*, Volume 101, pp. 99–111. A small number of businesses have had a futures capability, such as BT, see https://future.fandom.com/wiki/BT_Foresight_and_Futurology_Unit (Accessed 8 June 2020).

172 Hernandez, W. A. (2016). 'St. Augustine on Time' *International Journal of Humanities and Social Science*, 6(6), pp. 37–40.

173 Read more about Pythia at https://www.ancient-origins.net/myths-legends/pythia-oracle-delphi-001641 (Accessed 4 April 2020).

174 Townsend, P. and Gebhardt, J. (2007). *How Organisations Learn: Investigate, Identify, Institutionalise*, ASQ Quality Press.

175 Tsang, E. W. K. (1997) Organizational Learning and Learning Organization: A dichotomy between descriptive and prescriptive research, *Human Relations*, Vol. 50, No. 1, pp. 73–89.

176 Sahin, A.E. and Simsek, H. (1996), 'A qualitative assessment of organizational learning Processes in selected Turkish public and private high schools', paper presented at the Annual Meeting of the University Council for Educational Administration, Louisville, KY

177 Starkey, K., Tempest, S., and McKinlay (eds) (2004), *How Organizations Learn*, 2nd Edn. , Thompson.

178 Lipshitz, R., Friedman, V. and Popper, M. (2007) *Demystifying Organizational Learning*, California: Sage.

179 Diakopoulos, N. (2016). 'Accountability in algorithmic decision making', *Practice*. DOI https://doi.org/10.1145/2844110 (Accessed 11 July 2020).

180 Cheatham, B., Javanmardian, K., and Samandari, H. (2019). 'Confronting the risks of artificial intelligence', *McKinsey Quarterly*, April 2019. Retrieved from https://www.mckinsey.com/business-functions/mckinsey-analytics/our-insights/confronting-the-risks-of-artificial-intelligence. (Accessed 2 June 2020)

181 https://www.bloomberg.com/opinion/articles/2020-03-16/coronavirus-foreshadow-s-bigger-disruptions-in-future (Accessed 22 May 2020).

182 Schwab, K. (2017). *The Fourth Industrial Revolution*, World Economic Forum.

183 Mason, P. (2015). *PostCapitalism: A Guide to Our Future*, Penguin.

184 https://www.finder.com/uk/mobile-Internet-statistics (Accessed 2 June 2020).

185 Fry, H. (2018). *Hello World: How to be Human in the Age of the Machine*, W W Norton & Company and Susskind, R., and Susskind, D. (2017). *The Future of the Professions: How Technology Will Transform the Work of Human Experts*, Oxford University Press.

186 EY (2020). 'Beyond Covid-19: What will be the "new" normal?' available at https://assets.ey.com/content/dam/ey-sites/ey-com/fi_fi/pdf/beyond-covid-19-what-will-define-the-new-normal.pdf (Accessed 20 May 2020).

187 The Royal Society (2017). *Machine learning: the power and promise of computers that learn by example*. Available at https://royalsociety.org/~/media/policy/projects/machine-learning/publications/machine-learning-report.pdf (Accessed on 15 September 2019).

188 https://dictionary.cambridge.org/dictionary/english/instructions (Accessed 5 June 2020).

189 Goodfellow, I., Bengio, Y., and Courville, A. (2016). *Deep Learning*, MIT Press.

190 https://www.forbes.com/sites/louiscolumbus/2018/12/26/10-ways-machine-learning-is-revolutionizing-sales/#2a9fod993fd1 (24 January 2020).

191 Lee, B., Lessler, J., and Stuart, E. (2009). 'Improving Propensity Score Weighting Using Machine Learning', *Statistics in medicine*, 29, pp. 337–346. DOI 10.1002/sim.3782 (Accessed 17 May 2020). And Fry, H. (2018). *Hello World: How to be Human in the Age of the Machine*, W W Norton & Company.

192 The *Guardian* (22 May 2020). Available at https://www.theguardian.com/world/2020/may/21/just-7-per-cent-of-stockholm-had-covid-19-antibodies-by-end-of-april-study-sweden-coronavirus (Accessed 27 January 2020).

193 Jordan, M., and Mitchell, T. (2015). 'Machine learning: Trends, perspectives, and prospects'. *Science*, (6245), pp. 255–260. DOI 10.1126/science.aaa8415 (Accessed 18 May 2020).

194 For examples of chatbots and how they work, go to https://manychat.com/blog/chatbot-examples/ (Accessed 26 March 2020).

195 CIPD (2019). 'People and machines: from hype to reality' (7755), retrieved from https://www.cipd.co.uk/Images/people-and-machines-report-1_tcm18-56970.pdf (Accessed 29 June 2020).

196 Joh, E. (2017). 'Feeding the Machine: Policing, Crime Data, & Algorithms', *William & Mary Bill of Rights,* available at SSRN: https://ssrn.com/abstract=3020259 (Accessed 15 October 2019).

197 Harari, Y. (2017). *Homo Deus: A Brief History of Tomorrow.* Random House.

198 The *Guardian* (30 May 2020). Available at https://www.theguardian.com/technology/2020/may/30/microsoft-sacks-journalists-to-replace-them-with-robots

199 Deloitte. (2018). *Power Up: UK skills Boosting transferable skills to achieve inclusive growth and mobility,* retrieved from file:///C:/Users/mgtpharr/Downloads/deloitte-uk-power-up-uk-skills.pdf

200 Schwab, K., and Davis, N. (2018). *Shaping the Future of the Fourth Industrial Revolution,* Portfolio Penguin.

201 https://www.youtube.com/watch?v=5CO5eGoGINo for an explanation of Human Centric Analytics (Accessed 20 May 2020).

202 Acemoglu, D., and Restrepo, P. (2019). 'The Wrong Kind of AI? Artificial Intelligence and the Future of Labor Demand', *Cambridge Journal of Regions, Economy and Society,* available from https://economics.mit.edu/files/18782 (Accessed 20 May 2020).

203 https://www.ge.com/reports/game-augmented-reality-helping-factory-workers-become-productive/ (Accessed 25 August 2020).

204 https://www.mastercontrol.com/gxp-lifeline/3-things-you-need-to-know-about-industry-5.0/ (Accessed 23 July 2020) and Demir, K. A., Dövena, G., and Sezen, B. (2019). 'Industry 5.0 and Human-Robot Co-working'. *Procedia Computer Science,* pp. 158, 688–695.

205 Morgan, J. (2019). 'Will we work in twenty-first century capitalism? A critique of the fourth industrial revolution literature', *Economy and Society.* DOI https://doi.org/10.1080/03085147.2019.1620027 (Accessed 11 January 2020). And House of Lords Select Committee on Artificial Intelligence (2017). 'AI in the UK: ready, willing and able?'. Available at https://publications.parliament.uk/pa/ld201719/ldselect/ldai/100/100.pdf (Accessed 22 May 2020).

206 https://www.reuters.com/article/us-amazon-com-jobs-automation-insight/amazon-scraps-secret-ai-recruiting-tool-that-showed-bias-against-women-idUSKCN1MK08G (Accessed 2 July 2020).

207 Fuchs, D. (2018). 'The Dangers of Human-Like Bias in Machine-Learning Algorithms', *Missouri S&T's Peer to Peer* 2, 1. DOI https://scholarsmine. mst.edu/peer2peer/vol2/iss1/1 (Accessed 11 December 2019).

208 Read about a notorious product offer by Amazon at https://www.bbc. co.uk/news/technology-41320375 (Accessed 27 April 2020).

209 Zuboff, S. (2019). *The Age of Surveillance Capitalism*, Profile. Also read the interview with Zuboff at https://www.theguardian.com/technology/2019/ jan/20/shoshana-zuboff-age-of-surveillance-capitalism-google-facebook (Accessed 21 May 2020).

210 Collins, H. (2004). 'Interactional expertise as a third kind of knowledge'. *Phenomenology and the Cognitive Sciences*, 3, pp. 125–143.

211 Royakkers, L., Timmer, J., Kool, L., and van Est, R. (2018). 'Societal and ethical issues of digitization'. *Ethics and Information Technology*, 20(2), pp. 127–142. DOI 10.1007/s10676-018-9452-x (Accessed 12 July 2020).

212 Auluck, R. (2002) Benchmarking: A tool for facilitating Organisational Learning, Public Administration and Development, Vol. 22, No. 2, pp. 109–122.

213 Auluck, R. (2002) Benchmarking: A tool for facilitating Organisational Learning, Public Administration and Development, Vol. 22, No. 2, pp. 109–122.

214 Longbottom, D. (2000) Benchmarking in the UK: An empirical study of practitioners and academics, *Benchmarking: an International Journal*, Vol. 7, No. 2, pp. 98–117.

215 Pemberton, J. D., Stonehouse, G. H. and Yarrow, D. J. (2001) Benchmarking and the Role of Organisational Learning in Developing Competitive Advantage, *Knowledge and Process Management*, Vol. 8, No. 2, pp.123–135.

216 Zairi, M. (1998) *Effective management of benchmarking projects: Practical Guidelines and Examples*. Oxford: Butterworth-Heinemann.

217 Pemberton, J. D., Stonehouse, G. H. and Yarrow, D. J. (2001) Benchmarking and the Role of Organisational Learning in Developing Competitive Advantage, *Knowledge and Process Management*, Vol. 8, No. 2, pp.123–135.

218 Zairi, M. (1992) *Competitive Benchmarking: An Executive Guide*. Letchworth: Technical Communication Publishing.

219 Adapted from Bhutta, K. S. and Huq, F. (1999) Benchmarking: Best Approaches: an integrated approach, *Benchmarking: International Journal*, Vol. 6, Issue 3, pp. 254–268.

220 Hammer, M. and Champy, J. (1993) *Re-engineering the corporation: A Manifesto for Business Revolution*. London: Brealey.

221 Hutton, R. and Zairi, M. (1994) D2D: A Quality Winner's Approach to Benchmarking, *Benchmarking for Quality Management and Technology*, Vol. 1, No. 3, pp. 21–38.

311

222 Zairi, M. (1998) *Effective management of benchmarking projects: Practical Guidelines and Examples*. Oxford: Butterworth-Heinemann.

223 Dimovski, V. and Skerlavaj, M. (2004) Organizational Learning and Information-Communication Technologies - A Promising Link. Proceedings of Rijeka Faculty of Economics, *Journal of Economics and Business*, Vol. 22, No. 1, pp. 7–19, Available at SSRN: https://ssrn.com/abstract=2271493 (Accessed 2 October 2020).

224 Vandewalle, D., Ganesan, S., Challagalla, G. N., and Brown, S. P. (2000) 'An integrated model of feedback-seeking behavior: disposition, context and cognition'. *Journal of Applied Psychology*, Vol.85, No.6, pp. 996–1003.

225 https://www.inc.com/marcel-schwantes/elon-musk-shows-how-to-be-a-great-leader-with-what-he-calls-his-single-best-piece-of-advice.html (Accessed 21 October 2020).

226 Rouse, M. (2019). https://searchitchannel.techtarget.com/definition/feedback-loop (Accessed 4 July 2020).

227 Meyer, H. H., Kay, E., and French, J. R. P. (1965) 'Split roles in performance appraisal'. *Harvard Business Review*, Vol. 43, No. 1, January/February, pp. 123–9.

228 DeNisi, A. S., and Kluger, A. N. (2000) 'Feedback effectiveness: can 360-degree feedback be improved?'. *Academy of Management Executive*, Vol. 14, No. 1, pp. 129–39.

229 Qin, X., Ren, R., Zhang, Z-X., and Johnson, R. E. (2014). 'Fairness Heuristics and Substitutability Effects: Inferring the Fairness of Outcomes, Procedures, and Interpersonal Treatment When Employees Lack Clear Information'. *Journal of Applied Psychology*, 100(3), pp. 749–766.

230 Goldsmith, M. (2002). *'Try FeedForward Instead of Feedback'*. Available at: https://www.growthcoaching.com.au/articles-new/try-feedforward-instead-of-feedback?country=au (Accessed 23 October 2020).

231 Greeno, N. J. (2006). *Corporate Learning Strategies*. ASTD Press, p. 7.

232 Birch-Jensen, A., Gremyr, I., and Halldórsson, Á. (2020). 'Digitally connected services: Improvements through customer-initiated feedback'. *European Management Journal*. Available at https://doi.org/10.1016/j.emj.2020.03.008 (Accessed 17 October 2020).

233 Twersky, F., and Reichheld, F. (2019). 'Why Customer Feedback Tools Are Vital for Nonprofits'. *Harvard Business Review Digital Articles*, pp. 2–5.

234 Mayhew, E. (2019). 'Hearing everyone in the feedback loop: using the new discussion platform, Unitu, to enhance the staff and student dialogue'. *Eur Polit Sci* 18, pp. 714–728, available at https://doi.org/10.1057/s41304-019-00211-7 (Accessed 23 July 2020).

235 Galer, G., and Heijden, K. (1992). 'The Learning Organization: How Planners Create Organizational Learning', *Marketing Intelligence and Planning*, Vol. 10, No. 6, pp. 5–12.

236 Kolb, D. A. (2015). *Experiential Learning: Experience as the source of learning and development*. Pearson, FT Press.

237 Madzar, S. (1997). 'Hungry for feedback?' *Management Development Review*, Vol. 10, No. 6/7, pp. 246–248.

238 Garvin, D. (2000). *Learning in Action: A guide to putting the Learning Organizations to work*. Harvard Business School Press.
     9 Omachonu, V. K., and Ross, J. E (2003). *Principles of Total Quality*. CRC Press.
     9 Fundin, A. P., and Bergman, B. L. S (2003). 'Exploring the Customer Feedback Process'. *Measuring Business Excellence*, Vol. 7, No. 2, pp. 55–65.

239 Wirtz, J., Tambyah, S. K., and Mattila, A. S, (2010). 'Organizational learning from customer feedback received by service employees – a social capital perspective'. *Journal of Service Management*, Vol. 21, No. 3, pp. 363–387.

240 Argyris, C., and Schon, D. (1996). *Organizational Learning II: Theory, method and practice*. Addison Wesley.

241 Omachonu, V. K., and Ross, J. E (2003). *Principles of Total Quality*. CRC Press, p. 121.

242 Garvin, D. (2003). *Learning in Action: A guide to putting the Learning Organizations to work*. Harvard Business School Press.

243 Besieux, T. (2017). 'Why I hate feedback: Anchoring effective feedback within organizations'. *Business Horizons, 60*, pp. 435–439.

244 Eggers, J. P., and Suh, J. H. (2019). 'Experience and Behavior: How Negative Feedback in New Versus Experienced Domains Affects Firm Action and Subsequent Performance'. *Academy of Management Journal*, Vol. 62, No.2, pp. 309–334. DOI https://doi.org/10.5465/amj.2017.0046 (Accessed 29 May 2020).

245 Inspired by the seminal article – Crossan, M. M., Lane, H. W., and White, R. E. (1999). 'An Organizational Learning Framework: From Intuition to Institution.' *Academy of Management Review* 24 (3). pp. 522–537.

246 Jenkin, T. A. (2013). 'Extending the 4I Organizational Learning Model: Information Sources, Foraging Processes and Tools'. *Administrative Science*, Vol 3, pp. 96–109. DOI: 10.3390/admsci3030096 (Accessed 12 March 2020).

247 Wirtz, J., and Tomlin, M. (2000) 'Institutionalising customer-driven learning through fully integrated customer feedback system', *Managing Service Quality*, Vol. 10, No. 4, pp. 205–215.
     Musaji, S., Schulze, W. S., and De Castro, J. O. (2020). 'How Long Does It Take to Get to the Learning Curve?' *Academy of Management Journal*, 63(1),

pp. 205–223. DOI https://doi.org/10.5465/amj.2017.1145 (Accessed 30 March 2020).

Akbar, H., Baruch, Y., and Tzokas, N. (2018). 'Feedback Loops as Dynamic Processes of Organizational Knowledge Creation in the Context of the Innovations Front-end'. *British Journal of Management*, 29(3), pp. 445–463. DOI https://doi.org/10.1111/1467-8551.12251 (Accessed 10 July 2020).

248   https://global.llbean.com/ (Accessed 23 January 2020).

249   https://www.llbean.com/customerService/aboutLLBean/newsroom/ stories/20100914_Chris-Shares-Secrets-Top-Notch-Customer-Service. pdf (Accessed 17 February 2020).

250   Dixon N. M. (2017). *The Organizational Learning Cycle: How we can learn collectively*, Gower.

251   Greve, H. R., and Gaba, V (2020). 'Performance Feedback in Organizations and Groups: Common Themes', in Argote, L., and Levine, J. M. (2020). *The Oxford Handbook of Group and Organizational Learning*, Oxford University Press.

252   Szewczyk, K. (2019). 'Self-Assessment of an Organization According to the Polish Quality Award Modelon The Example Of An Automotive Company – Self-Assessment Process, Selected Improvement Actions'. *Management Sciences. Nauki o Zarządzaniu*, 24(1), pp. 48–57. DOI https:// doi.org/10.15611/ms.2019.1.06 (Accessed 20 June 2020).

253   National Student Survey (NSS). Available at https://www.thestudentsurvey. com/ (Accessed 18 July 2020).

254   Bourgeois, I., Whynot, J., and Thériault, É. (2015). 'Application of an organizational evaluation capacity self-assessment instrument to different organizations: Similarities and lessons learned'. *Evaluation and Program Planning*, VOL 50, Issue C, pp. 47–55. DOI https://doi.org/10.1016/j. evalprogplan.2015.01.004 (p.47) (Accessed 29 June 2020).

255   Hıdıroğlu, D. (2019). 'Self-assessment Performance Measurement in Construction Companies: An Application of the EFQM Excellence Model on Processes and Customer Stages'. *Procedia Computer Science*, 158, pp. 844–851. DOI https://doi.org/10.1016/j.procs.2019.09.122 (Accessed 5 February 2020).

256   Kalfa M., and Yetim, A. A. (2018). 'Organizational self-assessment based on common assessment framework to improve the organizational quality in public administration'. *Total Quality Management & Business Excellence*. DOI 10.1080/14783363.2018.1475223

257   Hussein, B., Mallcott, A., and Mikhridinova, N. (2019). 'Lessons learned from developing and applying self-assessment instruments for evaluating project management competences in two large organizations'. *Procedia*

Computer Science, 164, pp. 358–365. DOI https://doi.org/10.1016/j. procs.2019.12.194 (Accessed 1 August 2019).

258 Oakland, J. S. (1999). *Total Organizational Excellence: Achieving world-class performance*. Butterworth-Heinemann.

259 Dale, B., and Bunney, H. (1999). *Total Quality Management Blueprint*. Blackwell.

260 Hides, M. T., Davis, J., and Jackson, S. (2004). 'Implementation of EFQM excellence model self-assessment in UK higher education sector – Lessons learnt from other sectors'. *TQM Magazine*, Vol. 16, No. 13, pp. 194–201.

261 Lee, P. M., and Quazi, H. A. (2001). 'A methodology for developing a self-assessment tool to measure quality performance in organizations'. *International Journal of Quality and Reliability Management*, Vol. 18, No. 2, pp. 118–141.

262 Ford, M. W., and Evans, J. R. (2006). 'The role of follow-up in achieving results from self-assessment processes'. *International Journal of Quality & Reliability Management*, Vol. 23 No. 6, pp. 589–606. DOI https://doi. org/10.1108/02656710610672443 (Accessed 23 May 2020).

263 Auluck, R. (2002). 'Benchmarking: A tool for facilitating Organizational Learning'. *Public Administration and Development*, Vol. 22, No. 2, pp. 109–122.

264 Van der Wiele, T., Dale, B., and Williams, R. (2000). 'ISO 9000 series and excellence models: fad to fashion to fit'. *Journal of General Management*, Vol. 5, No. 3, pp. 50–66.

265 Nygaard, J., Colli, M., and Wæhrens, B. V. (2020). 'A self-assessment framework for supporting continuous improvement through IoT integration'. *Procedia Manufacturing*, 42, pp. 344–350. DOI https://doi. org/10.1016/j.promfg.2020.02.079 (Accessed 12 January 2020).

266 Szewczyk, K. (2019). 'Self-Assessment of an Organization According to the Polish Quality Award Modelon The Example Of An Automotive Company – Self-Assessment Process, Selected Improvement Actions'. *Management Sciences. Nauki o Zarządzaniu, 24*(1), pp. 48–57. DOI https:// doi.org/10.15611/ms.2019.1.06 (Accessed 5 March 2020).

267 https://www.gov.uk/government/publications/wuhan-novel-coronavirus-infection-prevention-and-control/introduction-and-organizational-preparedness (Accessed 14 June 2020) for UK government guidance. The Chartered Institute for Personnel and Development published an online example of risk assessment at work at https://www. cipd.co.uk/Images/general-workplace-safety-risk-assessment-example_tcm18-77042.pdf (Accessed 14 June 2020).

268 https://www.bsigroup.com/en-GB/topics/novel-coronavirus-covid-19/covid-19-guidelines/ (Accessed 29 July 2020).

269 Jeff Ellis & Associates, https://jellis.com/ (Accessed 17 May 2020).

270 Standard Operating Procedures.

271 Pitino, R., (2020). 'An American basketball coach who was the first head coach to win a men's National Collegiate Athletic Association (NCAA) Division I national championship with two different schools'. Available at https://www.britannica.com/biography/Rick-Pitino (Accessed 3 June 2020).

272 Laszlo, G. P., (1996). 'Quality Awards – Recognition or Model?'. *The TQM Magazine*, Vol. 8, No. 5, pp. 14–18.

273 Ghobadian, A., and Woo, H. S. (1996). 'Characteristics, benefits and shortcomings of four major quality awards'. *International Journal of Quality and Reliability Management*, Vol. 13, No. 2, pp. 10–44.

274 http://www.juse.or.jp/deming_en/award/ (Accessed 4 July 2020).

275 Stevenson, D. (1994). 'Quality Award – A means to an end or end in themselves?' *TQM Magazine*, Vol. 6, No. 5, pp. 7–8.

276 Jager, J. (1996). 'Promoting TQM through national quality awards – the Austrian experience'. *Managing Service Quality*, Vol. 6, No. 2, pp. 17–21.

277 Eriksson, H., (2003). 'Experience of working with in-company quality awards: A case study'. *The TQM Magazine*, Vol. 15, No. 6, pp. 397–407.

278 Stevenson, D. (1994). 'Quality Award – A means to an end or end in themselves?' *TQM Magazine*, Vol. 6, No. 5, pp. 7–8.

279 Wen, D. C., Dai, T., Chen, X., and Fu, T. (2017). 'A study on the economic benefits of the Government Quality Award in the Chinese context.' *Total Quality Management & Business Excellence*, 28(7/8), pp. 712–729. DOI https://doi.org/10.1080/14783363.2015.1114411 (Accessed 23 October 2020).

280 Weick K. E., and Westley F. (1996). 'Organizational Learning: Affirming an Oxymoron', in Clegg, S. R, Hardy, C., and Nod, W. R (2013). *Handbook of Organizational Studies*, Sage (p. 456).

281 Mann, R. (2018). 'Latest research reveals 55 countries have a Business Excellence Award'. DOI https://blog.bpir.com/business-excellence/latest-research-reveals-55-countries-have-a-business-excellence-award (Accessed 27 June 2020).

282 EFQM (2020). DOI https://www.efqm.org/index.php/efqm-model/ (Accessed 4 April 2020).

283 Crossan, M., Lane, H. W and White, R. E. (1999). 'Organizational Learning Framework: from Intuition to Institution'. *Academy of Management Review*, Vol. 24, No. 3, pp. 522–537, 524.

284 Drucker, P. (2011). *Managing in Turbulent Times*. Routledge, p.24.

285 https://www.sideways6.com/ (Accessed 25 July 2020).

286 https://www.gov.uk/expenses-and-benefits-employee-suggestion-schemes (Accessed 30 March 2020).

287 Milner, E., Kinnel, M., and Usherwood, B. (1995). 'Employee suggestion systems; a management tool for 1990s'. *Library Management*, Vol. 16, No. 3, pp. 3–8.

288 Carpenter, W.W, (1930). 'The Suggestion System'. *Peabody Journal of Education*, Vol.8, No.1, pp. 13–15.

289 Birkinshaw, J. (2013). 'Employee-led Innovation'. Available at https://www.london.edu/think/employee-led-innovation (Accessed 20 February 2020).

290 Pedler, M., and Aspinwall, K. (1998) *A Concise Guide to the Learning Organization*,. Lemos and Crane.

291 Cooley, R. E., Helbling, C., and Fuller, U. D. (2001). 'Knowledge, organization and suggestion schemes'. *Management of Industrial and Corporate Knowledge*, No. 1, pp. 47–56.

292 Greeno, N. J. (2006). *Corporate Learning Strategies*. ASTD Press.

293 Ideas UK (2020). DOI https://www.ideasuk.com/ (Accessed 17 June 2020).

294 Deming, W. E. (2000). *Out of the Crisis*. Cambridge Press.

295 Read more at https://www.referenceforbusiness.com/encyclopedia/Str-The/Suggestion-Systems.html#ixzz6QEQNyJG8 (Accessed 23 June 2020).

296 Du Plessis, A. J. (2016). 'The Contribution of Policies, Procedures and Rules for Successful Suggestion Systems in Organizations: Some Research Findings'. *Journal of Community Positive Practices*, 16(1), pp. 92–106.

297 Santos, G., Afonseca, J., Lopes, N., Félix, M. J., and Murmura, F. (2018). 'Critical success factors in the management of ideas as an essential component of innovation and business excellence'. *International Journal of Quality and Service Sciences*, Vol. 10, No. 3, pp. 214–232. DOI https://doi.org/10.1108/IJQSS-05-2017-0051 (Accessed 20 October 2020).

298 Faragher, J. (2013). 'Creating an employee suggestion scheme that delivers'. Available at https://www.personneltoday.com/hr/creating-an-employee-suggestion-scheme-that-delivers/ (Accessed 10 May 2020).

299 Toyota (2014). 'Toyota and the Power of Suggestion'. Available at https://blog.toyota.co.uk/toyota-and-the-power-of-suggestion (Accessed 15 March 2020).

300 Scilla Elworthy founded Oxford Research Group in 1982, to promote effective dialogue between nuclear weapons policy-makers and their opponents. Source https://www.ted.com/speakers/scilla_elworthy (Accessed 24 June 2020).

301 Andersen, H. L. (n.d.). 'Organizational dialogue: A conceptual framework for an interdisciplinary understanding'. DOI https://www.academia.edu/21910228/Organizational_dialogue_A_conceptual_framework_for_an_interdisciplinary_understanding (Accessed 3 February 2020).

302 https://www.merriam-webster.com/dictionary/dialogue (Accessed 20 October 2020).

303 Dixon N. M. (1999) *The Organisational Learning Cycle: How we can learn collectively*, 2nd edn. Gower. p.110.

304 EFQM Excellence Model (2015). DOI https://www.qualityscotland. co.uk/sites/default/files/efqm/EFQMpercent20Excellenceper cent20Modelpercent20Bookpercent202013.pdf (Accessed 20 May 2019).

305 https://www.mckinsey.com/business-functions/organization/our-insights/a-leaders-guide-communicating-with-teams-stakeholders-and-communities-during-covid-19, for McKinsey's guide for leaders (Accessed 26 June 2020).

306 http://scihi.org/communication-paul-watzlawick/ (Accessed 21 October 2020).

307 Madzar, S. (1997) *Hungry for feedback?* Management Development Review. Vol. 10, No. 6/7, pp. 246–248.

308 Maurer, M., (2008). 'Dialogue as Organizational Learning Interventions: Taking a closer look at psychological barriers'. DOI https://files.eric. ed.gov/fulltext/ED501668.pdf (Accessed 4 February 2020).

309 Senge, P. (1990). *The Fifth Discipline: The Art and Practice of the Learning Organization*. Random House.

310 Ibid, p. 243.

311 Brockbank, A., McGill, I., and Beech, N., (eds) (2002). *Reflective Learning in Practice*. Gower, pp. 26–28.

312 'Using Dialogue as a Tool in the Organizational Change Process'. *California Tomorrow*. Available at http://www.mpassociates.us/ uploads/3/7/1/0/37103967/dialoguemaggiepotachukhandout.pdf (Accessed 10 March 2020).

313 Toulmin, S. (1958). *The Uses of Argument*. Cambridge University Press, Go to https://owl.purdue.edu/owl/general_writing/academic_writing/ historical_perspectives_on_argumentation/toulmin_argument.html (Accessed 24 October 2020) for a detailed example of Toulmin's box diagram.

314 Mason, R. O., and Mitroff, I. (1981). *Challenging Strategic Planning*, Wiley.

315 Lane, A. B. (2020). 'The dialogic ladder: Toward a framework of dialogue'. *Public Relations Review*, 46(1). DOI https://doi.org/10.1016/j. pubrev.2019.101870 (Accessed 2 July 2020).

316 Harmon, J., Kowalski, R., & Kowalski, D. (2018). A Contextual Mapping Intervention for Organization Dialogue and Change. *OD Practitioner*, 50(1), pp. 13–21.

317 Visser, F. S., Stappers P. J., Van der Lugt, R. and Sanders, E. B-N, (2005). 'Contextmapping: experiences from practice, CoDesign'. *International Journal of CoCreation in Design and the Arts*, Vol. 1 No. 2, pp. 119–149. DOI: 10.1080/15710880500135987 (Accessed 1 July 2020).

318 'Basics of Contextmapping'. DOI http://contextmapping.com/basics/ (Accessed 30 May 2020).

319 Internal Document (n.d.). 'Assessors' Feedback Report'.

320 Argyris, C., and Schon, D. (1996) *Organizational Learning II: Theory, method and practice*. Addison Wesley.

321 https://www.ipsos.com/en/mystery-shopping-0 (Accessed 3 July 2020).

322 Peterman, K., and Young, D. (2015). 'Mystery Shopping: An Innovative Method for Observing Interactions With Scientists During Public Science Events'. *Visitor Studies*, 18:1, pp. 83–102. DOI 10.1080/10645578.2015.1016369 (Accessed 10 July 2020).

323 https://www.performanceinpeople.co.uk/mystery-shopping/ (Accessed 4 July 2020).

324 MSPA (2018). *Mystery Shopping – How Big is The Market*. DOI https://www.mspa-ea.org/news/newsitem/58-mystery-shopping-how-big-is-the-market.html (Accessed 13 June 2020).

325 M., A. S. R. (2019) 'The Dimensions of Mystery Shopping Program (DMSP) – Checklist Construction'. *International Journal of Management, Accounting & Economics*, 6(5), pp. 440–452. DOI http://search.ebscohost.com/login.aspx?direct=true&db=bth&AN=137734911&site=eds-live (Accessed 19 June 2020).

326 Sambronska, K. (2018). 'Mystery Shopping – a Tool for Measuring the Satisfaction of Guests in Accommodation Services'. *International Multidisciplinary Scientific Conference on Social Sciences & Arts SGEM*, 5, pp. 687–692. DOI 10.5593/sgemsocial2018/1.3. (Accessed 15 March 2020).

327 https://www.ipsos.com/sites/default/files/2017-07/IpsosLoyalty_DesigningSmarterMysteryShoppingProgam.pdf (Accessed 10 June 2020).

328 Durugy, A., and Kollar, P. (2017). 'On the Use of Mystery Shopping to Measure Competences'. *Journal of HRM*, 20(1), pp. 81–88. DOI http://search.ebscohost.com/login.aspx?direct=true&db=bth&AN=123285305&site=eds-live (Accessed 19 June 2020).

329 Blessing, G., and Natter, M. (2019). 'Do Mystery Shoppers Really Predict Customer Satisfaction and Sales Performance?' *Journal of Retailing*, Volume 95, Issue 3, pp. 47–62. DOI https://doi.org/10.1016/j.jretai.2019.04.001.

330 PWC (2020). 'What is an Audit?'. DOI https://www.pwc.com/m1/en/services/assurance/what-is-an-audit.html (Accessed 20 May 2020).

331 ASQ (2020). 'What is Auditing?'. DOI https://asq.org/quality-resources/auditing. (Accessed 18 May 2020).

332 'ISO 19011:2018 Guidelines for auditing management systems'. International Organization for Standardization. DOI https://www.iso.org/standard/70017.html (Accessed 12 May 2020).

333 Walker, C. (2014). 'Organizational Learning: The Role of Third Party Auditors in Building Compliance and Enforcement Capability.' *International Journal of Auditing*, 18, pp. 213–222. DOI 10.1111/ijau.12026 (Accessed 11 June 2020).

334 Causholli, M. (2016). 'Evidence of Organizational Learning and Organizational Forgetting from Financial Statement Audits.' *Auditing: A Journal of Practice & Theory*, 35 (2), pp. 53–72. DOI 10.2308/ajpt-51267 (Accessed 17 June 2020).

335 Rains, D. (2020). 'Audits are a good thing'. DOI https://vividlearningsystems.com/blog/audits-are-a-good-thing (Accessed 15 June 2020).

336 The *Guardian* (2020). DOI https://www.theguardian.com/environment/2020/apr/20/deepwater-horizon-10-years-later-could-it-happen-again. (Accessed 30 April 2020).

337 Ajaxa, L. (2020). 'How Does Audit Help in Decision Making?' Available at https://www.jaxaauditors.com/blog/how-does-audit-help-in-decision-making (Accessed 2 June 2020).

338 Jacob, R., Madu, C. N. and Tang, C. (2004). 'An Empirical Assessment of the Financial Performance of Malcolm Baldrige Award Winners'. *International Journal of Quality & Reliability Management*, Vol. 21, No 8, pp. 897–914.

339 Peters, J. (1997). 'Operationalising Total Quality', in Mumford, A. (1997) *Action Learning at Work*, Gower (Ed).

340 Garvin, D. (2000). *Learning in Action: A guide to putting the Learning Organizations to work*. Harvard Business School Press.

341 McAdam, R., Leitch, C., and Harrison, R. (1998). 'The links between organizational learning and total quality: critical review'. *Journal of European Industrial Training*, Vol. 22, No. 2, pp. 47–56.

342 We assume that Organizational Excellence is a natural evolution of Total Quality or the next phase of its development; the said assumption is supported by the literature related to the establishment of excellence awards and models such as the EFQM Model and the Deming Prize.

343 Higan, A. (1998). 'Organizational Learning: Approach to Building Learning Organizations' (in Arabic). *Public Administration*, Vol. 37, No. 4, pp. 675–712.

344 This chapter is based on the work of Garad and Gold (2019) (see below).

345 Garad, A., and Gold, J. (2019). 'The learning-driven organization: toward an integrative model for Organizational learning'. *Industrial and Commercial Training*, Vol. 51, No. 6, pp. 329–341. DOI https://doi.org/10.1108/ICT-10-2018-0090 (Accessed 18 July 2020).

346 Argyris, C., and Schon, D. (1978). *Organizational Learning: A theory of action perspective*. Addison Wesley.

Argyris, C. (1996). 'Towards a comprehensive theory of management'. In Moingeon, B., and Edmondson, A. (eds). *Organizational Learning and Competitive Advantage*. Sage.

Fioretti, G. (2007). 'The Organizational Learning Curve'. *European Journal for Operational Research*, Vol. 177, No. 3, pp. 1375–1384.

Garratt, B. (2000). *The Learning Organization: Developing democracy at work*. Harper Collins Business.

347 Argote, L. (2013). *Organizational learning: Creating, retaining and transferring knowledge*. Springer Science Business Media.

Lipshitz, R., Friedman, V., J., and Popper, M. (2007). *Demystifying Organizational Learning*. Sage.

348 Harari, Y. N. (2017). *Homo Deus: A Brief History of Tomorrow*. Vintage.

349 Harari, Y. N. (2017). *Homo Deus: A Brief History of Tomorrow*. Vintage.

350 Details at http://www.efqm.org/what-we-do/assessment/self-assessment (Accessed 20 February 2019).

351 Nonaka, I., and Takeuchi, H. (1995). 'The Knowledge-Creating Company: How Japanese Companies Create the Dynamics of Innovation'. Oxford University Press.

Saadat, V., and Saadat, Z. (2016). 'Organizational Learning as a Key Role of Organizational Success'. *Procedia – Social and Behavioural Sciences*, No. 230, pp. 219–225.

352 Chiva, R., Alegre, J., and Lapiedra, R. (2007). 'Measuring organizational learning capability among the workforce'. *International Journal of Manpower*, Vol. 28, No. 3/4, pp. 224–242.

353 Guță. A. L. (2014). 'Measuring organizational learning. Model testing in two Romanian universities'. *Management & Marketing. Challenges for the Knowledge Society*, Vol. 9, No. 3, pp. 253–282.

354 Crossan, M., Lane, H., and White, R. (1999). 'An organizational learning framework: from intuition to institution'. *Academy of Management Review*, Vol. 24 No. 3, pp. 522–537.

355 Bontis, N., Crossan, M. M., and Hulland, J. (2002). 'Managing an organizational learning system by aligning stocks and flows'. *Journal of Management Studies*, Vol. 39, No. 4, pp. 437–469.

356 Templeton, G. F., Lewis, B. R., and Snyder, C. A. (2002). 'Development of a Measure for Organizational Learning Construct'. *Journal of Management Information Systems*, Vol. 19, No. 2 pp. 175–218.

357 Putz, D., Schilling, J., Kluge, A., and Stangenberg, C. (2012). 'Measuring organizational learning from errors: Development and validation of an integrated model and questionnaire'.

358 Senge, P. (2006). *The Fifth Discipline: The Art and Practice of the Learning Organization* (2nd ed.). New York: Doubleday/Currency.

359 Dixon N. M. (1999). *The Organizational Learning Cycle: How we can learn collectively*. Gower.

360 Lipshitz, R., Friedman, V. J. and Popper, M. (2007). *Demystifying Organizational Learning*, Sage Publications; Argote L. (2013) 'Organization Learning: A Theoretical Framework'. In: *Organizational Learning*. Springer, Boston, MA. https://doi.org/10.1007/978-1-4614-5251-5_2 (Accessed 24 October 2020)

361 Chiva, R., Alegre, J. and Lapiedra, R. (2007), 'Measuring organisational learning capability among the workforce', *International Journal of Manpower*, Vol. 28 No. 3/4, pp. 224–242. https://doi.org/10.1108/01437720710755227. (Accessed 26 October 2020); Crossan, M., Lane, H., and White, R. (1999). 'An organizational learning framework: from intuition to institution'. *Academy of Management Review*, Vol. 24 No. 3, pp. 522–537.

362 Jyothibabu, C., Farooq, A., and Pradhan, B. B. (2010). 'An integrated scale for measuring an organizational learning system'. *The Learning Organization*, Vol. 17, No. 4, pp. 303–327.

363 Antonacopoulou, E. (2006), 'Learning-in-practise: the social complexity of learning in working life'. AIM working paper series, Advanced Institute of Management Research, London.

364 DiBella, A. & Nevis, E. (1998) *How Organizations Learn: An Integrated Strategy for Building Learning Capability*. San Francisco: Jossey-Bass.

365 Weick K.E., and Westley F. (1996), Organizational Learning: Affirming an Oxymoron, In Clegg, S.R, Hardy, C., and Nod, W.R, *Handbook of Organizational Studies* pp. 440–458, London: Sage.

366 Cook, S., and Yanow, D. (1993) 'Culture and Organizational Learning'. In M. Cohen and L. Sproull (eds) *Organizational Learning*, pp. 430–459. Thousand Oaks, CA: Sage Publications.

367 Schein, E. H. (2004). 'Organizational Culture and Leadership' Wiley and Son.

368 Senge, P. (2006). *The Fifth Discipline: The Art and Practice of the Learning Organization* (2nd ed.). New York: Doubleday/Currency.

369 Yang, B., Watkins, K. E., & Marsick, V. J. (2004). The construct of the learning organization: dimensions, measurement, and validation. *Human*

Resource Development Quarterly, pp. 15, 31–55. DOI 10.1002/hrdq.1086 (Accessed 19 October 2020).

Banerjee, P. Gupta, R., and Bates, R. (2017). 'Influence of Organizational Learning Culture on Knowledge Worker's Motivation to Transfer Training: Testing Moderating Effects of Learning Transfer Climate'. *Current Psychology*, Vol. 36, No. 3, pp. 606–617.

370 Friedman, V. J., Lipshitz, R., and Overmeer, W. (2001). 'Creating Conditions for Organizational Learning' in Edited by Meinolf Dierkes, M., Antal, A.B., Child, J. and Nonaka, I. (2001). *Handbook of Organizational Learning and Knowledge*. Oxford University Press.

371 Garvin, D. A. (1993). 'Building a learning organization'. *Harvard Business Review*, Vol. 71, No. 4, pp. 78–91.

372 Rebelo, T. M., and Gomes, A. D. (2011). 'Conditioning factors of an organizational learning culture'. *Journal of Workplace Learning*, Vol. 23, No. 3, pp. 173–194. DOI https://doi.org/10.1108/13665621111117215 (Accessed 1 May 2020).

373 Marquardt, M. J. (2002). *Building The Learning Organization*, McGraw Hill.

374 Malik, M. E., Rizwan, Q. D., and Ali, U. (2011). 'Impact of motivation to learn and job attitudes on organizational learning culture in a public service organization of Pakistan'. *African Journal of Business Management*, Vol. 5, No. 3, pp. 844–854.

375 Jo, S., and Joo, B. (2011). 'Knowledge sharing: the influences of learning organization culture, organizational commitment and organizational citizenship behaviors'. *Journal of Leadership & Organizational Culture*, Vol. 18, No. 3, pp. 353–364.

376 Islam, T., Ahmed, I., and Ahmad, U.N.U, (2015). 'The influence of organizational learning culture and perceived organizational support on employees' affective commitment and turnover intention'. *Nankai Business Review International*, Vol. 6, No. 4, pp. 417–431. DOI https://doi.org/10.1108/NBRI-01-2015-0002 (Accessed 4 December 2019).

377 Friedman, V. J., Lipshitz, R., and Overmeer, W. (2001). 'Creating Conditions for Organizational Learning' in Edited by Meinolf Dierkes, M., Antal, A.B., Child, J. and Nonaka, I. (2001). *Handbook of Organizational Learning and Knowledge*. Oxford University Press.

378 Mitki, Y., Shani, A. B., and Stjernberg, T. (2008). 'Leadership Development and Learning Mechanisms System Transformation as a Balancing Act'. *Leadership and Organization Development Journal*, Vol. 29, pp. 68–84.

379 Cirella, S., Ganterino, F., Guerci, M., and Shani, A. (2016). 'Organizational Learning Mechanisms and Creative Climate: Insights from an Italian Fashion Design Company'. *Journal for Creativity and Innovation Management*, Vol. 25, No. 2, pp 211–222.

380 Shani, A. B., and Docherty, P. (2008). 'Learning by Design: Key Mechanisms in Organization Development'. In Cummings, T. (Ed.) (2008). *Handbook of Organizational Change and Development*. Sage, Thousand Oaks.

381 Wilhelm, W. (2005). 'Learning Architectures: Building Organizational and Individual Learning'. GCA Press.

382 Argyris, C. (1996). 'Towards a comprehensive theory of management'. In Moingeon, B., and Edmondson, A. (eds) *Organizational Learning and Competitive Advantage*. Sage.

383 Blindenbacher, R. and Nashat, B. (2012). 'The Governmental Learning Spiral: A concept to organize governmental learning around complex governance challenges.' Institute for Research and Debate on Governance, Charles Léopold Mayer Publishing House. Available at http://www.institut-gouvernance.org/docs/the_governmental_learning_spiral.pdf (Accessed 1 June 2020).

384 https://www.vuca-world.org/ (Accessed 23 June 2020).

385 Snowden, D. J., Boone, M. (2007). 'A Leader's Framework for Decision Making'. *Harvard Business Review*, November 2007, pp. 69–76.

386 Paris Declaration on Aid Effectiveness OECD (Organization for Economic Co-operation and Development). 2005. DOI http://www.oecd.org/dataoecd/11/41/34428351.pdf (Accessed 10 April 2020).

ACKNOWLEDGEMENTS

We want to thank the Bloomsbury team, who have supported and guided us throughout the process. Thanks to our families; we could not have completed this book without their support. Special thanks also to the interviewees at the organizations mentioned in this book, our students, colleagues and mentors. Thank you to our reviewers who encouraged us and expressed their views; special thanks to Dr Edward de Bono and Professor Edgar Schein. And a big thank you to our dear reader for whom we wrote this book.